I Need This Mountain to Move

I Need This Mountain To Move
From Stuck to Unstoppable!
Discovering the Power to ~~See Mountains~~ Move Mountains.

Moving Mountains Series Book One

Kelvin Pendleton

First edition paperback published 2024
Kelvin Pendleton, LLC
The Pendleton Development Team

Names from personal stories have been omitted to respect the privacy of individuals.

Copyright © 2024 by Kelvin Pendleton. First edition paperback 2024.

All rights reserved. No part of this publication may be reproduced, distributed, or transmitted in any form or by any means, including photocopying, recording, or other electronic or mechanical methods, without the prior written permission of the publisher, except in the case of brief quotations embodied in critical reviews and certain other noncommercial uses permitted by copyright law.

ISBN 979-8-9910469-0-9 (paperback) | ISBN 979-8-9910469-1-6 (hardcover)

This publication is designed to provide accurate and authoritative information regarding the subject matter covered. It is sold with the understanding that neither the author nor the publisher is engaged in rendering counseling, coaching, or other professional services through this publication. The advice and strategies contained herein may not be suitable for your situation. You should consult with a professional when appropriate. Neither the publisher nor the author shall be liable for any loss of profit or any other commercial damages, including but not limited to special, incidental, consequential, personal, or other damages.

Cover photo by Leio McLaren by Unsplash.
Cover designed by Kelvin Pendleton of The Pendleton Development Team.
Chapter photos/Unsplash per its usage license, terms, and conditions.
Author photo by Aliaks Klyshevich.
Edited by Kelvin Pendleton.

Scripture quotations taken from The Holy Bible, New International Version® NIV® Copyright © 1973, 1978, 1984, 2011 by Biblica, Inc. Used with permission. All rights reserved worldwide.

Scripture quotations marked HCSB are taken from the Holman Christian Standard Bible®, Used by Permission HCSB ©1999,2000,2002,2003,2009 Holman Bible Publishers. Unless directly quoted, referenced verses are paraphrased in the author's voice.

Published in 2024 by Kelvin Pendleton, LLC
d/b/a The Pendleton Development Team
www.kelvinpendleton.com | books@kelvinpendleton.com

Printed in the United States of America

Dedication

This is my first published book and is, first and foremost, dedicated to Abba, my heavenly father. I also dedicate this book to my parents, Elijah and Barbara Pendleton, my beautiful wife, Alisa Pendleton, and my wonderful children, Joshua and Gabrielle. They are all my inspiration, and I love them with all my being.

Table of Contents

Preface 9

Chapter 1: Pardon me? 17

Chapter 2: The Power of Prayer 37

Chapter 3: The Power of Petitions 53

Chapter 4: The Power of Patience 71

Chapter 5: The Power of Perseverance 89

Chapter 6: The Power that Moves Mountains 105

Acknowledgments 123

About the Author 124

"Self-awareness is our capacity to stand apart from ourselves and examine our thinking, our motives, our history, our scripts, our actions, and our habits."

Stephen R. Covey

Preface

We often use the mountain metaphor to represent challenges in our lives that we find too difficult to overcome. Naturally, we cannot walk up to a mountain and push it out of our way. Therefore, saying that we have mountains in our lives indicates that our challenges, obstacles, and problems are insurmountable and overwhelming. Mountains can block our view, stand in our way, hinder us from going forward, or cause us to doubt that we can reach our destination. Our unfortunate response is that we feel stuck, overwhelmed, and often give up because we feel it is impossible to move forward. But what if there was a way to figure out why we feel stuck and develop a plan to move forward? I am so glad you asked that question! After reading this book, I hope you will feel encouraged to analyze your mountain, develop a plan, execute the plan, and move past the mountain in your life. If achieving that dream or goal or overcoming that challenge or problem will bring positive results, it is worth fighting for. It is worth fighting for because you deserve to live a life of victory and success.

However, one of the reasons we do not live a life of victory and success is that we see the goal or problem and try to tackle it head-on; in most cases, that is what we are taught to do. We are taught to face our fears, fight through our problems, conquer our challenges, and reach our goals by any means necessary. So, we endeavor to do those things and often face difficulties and failures. Usually, this is because we didn't take the time to analyze what we were dealing with and develop a plan of action to help us move forward. Inasmuch, tackling things head-on is where experience can be an ally or our worst enemy.

I say that because experience will lead us to believe we can handle things on the fly. We tell ourselves that we can do it again if we have done it before. In most cases, feeling that we can repeat our success is accurate because we face the same challenge or accomplish the same goal. But what happens when life happens? That is when life will make you feel you are about to hit a home run from the fastball you are expecting, but instead, life throws you a curve ball, and you experience a swing and a miss. In that moment, anxious feelings can arise and make us feel we do not know what to do. You already have two strikes, so the next strike means you're out. Well, even in this sports analogy I am using, there is the option of taking time out so that coaches can confer and implement a strategy for what to do next.

Therefore, we will spend some time with a spiritually practical approach that you can use to navigate the mountains in your life. You would be surprised at how sometimes the mountain hinders you because of a few simple challenges that were not thought of before. Think about it; let's say you want to climb a mountain. If you've never done it before, you could try to go and try to climb it, but that could be a fatal mistake. However, if you take the time to research what is needed, confer with others who have climbed a mountain before, and assess if you are physically able to climb the mountain, you can increase your chances of success. You may have learned about climbing gear, clothes, and strategies that help you climb the mountain. Then, you execute what you've learned; before you know it, you are celebrating on top of that mountain!

Excellent job! Now, let's say we choose another mountain to climb. This is where I mentioned that experience can be our worst enemy. Because we can feel at this point that we've climbed a mountain before and have the tools necessary to climb, we should be able to climb any mountain. But what if this new mountain takes you to a higher altitude? Are you prepared to deal with colder temperatures or reduced oxygen levels? Do you have tools in the event you encounter ice? Some mountains have one temperature environment at the foot of the mountain, but the mountain's crest can be completely different. Thus, if we try to climb the mountain without a new assessment, the confidence we gain from experience can cause us to fail.

With each new goal, dream, challenge, or problem, we need to treat them as individuals and not use a blanket plan to accomplish or overcome each one. In addition, take a moment after each victory and success to learn from what you encountered. Be sure to look out for my book, "Good Problems," because there you will learn that not all problems are bad for you. Some problems and challenges will be a great blessing to your life because they can instill character, growth, and mental toughness in your life. Therefore, overcoming that mountain gives you more strength and endurance to face the next one. That is why you should not be afraid when you have a mountain in your life; surmounting the mountain will give you more than you expected in your life. But it all starts with your desire to need the mountain to move. I say that because I already believe that you can get your mountain to move. But just because that is what I believe doesn't mean your mountains will move. Mountains move when you believe it for yourself.

Let's Put The Work In

As you continue to read this book, I hope you are not just reading this recreationally. Instead, I encourage you to take the time to think and reflect on what is being shared. This book may not cover all the factors that make us feel stuck, but it will lay a solid foundation and start the conversation through self-awareness. This self-awareness will help you assess why you are facing a mountain. In other words, this book is not a fix; it's a tool to help you create a conversational blueprint to move mountains. Each chapter will present an affirmation for you to use based on the topic and action steps, which will give you questions to guide you through your thoughts. Before moving on to the next chapter in this book, please take a moment to think about your mountain and why you feel you may be feeling stuck. If you have more than one mountain that needs to move, focus on just one for now. Focusing on more than one at a time can hinder your success.

To take things to another level, use this information as a guide, and then create your own affirmations, action steps, and prayer. Make it your own and enhance your personal and spiritual growth. If you have the companion journal, you can use it to complete this. If you do not have the journal, why not? Just kidding. You can write your thoughts using a notebook, paper, or journal. When answering questions for each principle, it may help to read reputable books on that subject to help you understand what can be done for you to self-analyze on that topic. For instance, if you read the chapter on forgiveness, you may want to find books that go deeper into how to forgive. You can also view the website for this book at books.kelvinpendleton.com for resources related to this book. So, let's put the work in so we can move these mountains!

Affirmation:

I am going to get unstuck.

I am going to move forward.

My mountain is not going to hold me back.

And I am going to experience victory and success.

Action Steps:

Once you have focused on what is your mountain, ask yourself these questions:

1. Why do I feel this is a mountain in my life?
2. What have I already done to try to surmount this mountain?
3. Does this mountain make me feel stuck, anxious, and afraid, or is surmounting the mountain impossible?
4. What do I feel is hindering me from moving forward?
5. Have I ever consulted help with this mountain? Has it been with someone who has faced the same mountain?
6. Do I have someone in my life who can hold me accountable for moving forward past this mountain, someone who can keep me motivated and guided until I succeed?

"Forgiveness is unlocking the door to set someone free and realizing you were the prisoner!"

Max Lucado

Chapter 1: Pardon me?

As we journey through the discussion of getting mountains to move in our lives, we will analyze different topics and how they compare to our lives. Self-examination is essential in getting mountains to move because it helps us understand what is necessary when taking the next step. When I was a kid, I would ask my parents about Santa around Christmas time. No matter my question, they had a clever answer that satisfied my curiosity. After all, I grew up in Miami, Florida, and we did not have a chimney, so how did he get in right? First, it was, "We let him in when he arrives." Then, "He gets to everyone in one night using semi-trucks to help deliver." It helped that I heard trucks driving through the neighborhood that night.

Well, one year, my brother and I decided to stay up to see what happens. We tried keeping each other up but to no avail. We finally fell asleep and did not see any action. Shortly after, I woke up and ran to the Christmas tree. To my surprise, guess what I saw? Absolutely nothing. There was not a single gift under the tree. Perplexed, I ran to my parents' room and woke them up, explaining that the tree was empty. Their first response was, "Maybe he hasn't come yet." Okay, so I ran back to the living room, gazed out the window, and saw kids on bicycles, skateboards, and roller skates. Other kids with remote control cars. Yes, these were the days when kids played outside, which is rare today. Anyway, I returned to my parent's room and explained what I saw.

Their next response was, "Well, you know how the story goes. He checks his list to find out who's naughty or nice." Perplexed once again, I ran back into the living room. I stared at the tree momentarily, then gazed out the window again. It was Christmas, and I had no toys under the tree this year. I dropped to the floor underneath the window, still able to hear kids playing outside. I pressed my back against the wall and folded my legs to bring my knees to my chest. Tears began to form as I tried to figure out what I had done to be on the naughty list. I don't know how long I sat there, but I remember reviewing the previous year in my head. Did I have arguments? Did I mistreat someone? What could it be?

No matter how much I reviewed my actions, I could not think of anything. So, I decided to go to a reputable source who would know what I did to be on the naughty list: my parents. So, I wiped the tears and ran back into their room. As I walked into their room this time, I found them laughing. Now, who could laugh at a time like this? I asked what was so funny, and that was when they pointed to their bedroom closet and told me to look in there. And lo and behold, the closet was filled with gifts! Wait, did Santa choose the closet instead of the tree? My parents responded, "We fell asleep waiting for y'all to go to bed. We didn't have time to put the presents under the tree!" The truth was clear: Santa was my parents, and they pulled a diabolical trick on me that would last a lifetime.

But not in the way you may be thinking. You may think that I harbored ill feelings towards them because of what they did or was traumatized. But instead, I recognized that it was my behavior that led them to their actions. As harsh as it felt, if I had done what I was supposed to, they would have been able to do what they were supposed to. The lifetime effect of this event is that at the end of the year, I take a moment to do a self-reflection. I review challenges, arguments, mistakes, broken relationships, etc. Then, I consider what I could have done to avoid those things. Then, after reflecting on the losses, I reflect upon the wins. I celebrate the progress I've made and give thanks to God for all the wins and for helping me through the losses. Thus, I have experienced self-examination for most of my life, which keeps me growing.

However, buried within that, self-examination and the experience with my parents are essential concepts. In addition to what I did wrong to others and seeking forgiveness from them, what about those moments when someone did something to me? Have they taken the time to ask for my forgiveness? This is part of my annual self-check-up to ensure I am not harboring ill feelings about what someone has done to me. Sometimes, I realized what I was doing but did not realize how it had impacted my life. See, I was physically assaulted by those I considered to be my friends, and it left me with trust issues every time someone tried to get close to me to build a friendship. Thus, my life was changing not because of the event but because of my lack of pardon.

So, let's take a moment to dive into the importance of self-examination and ensure that we release any harbored unforgiveness that may weigh heavily upon our hearts. We have mountains that need to be moved, and in my case, my mountain was the challenge of building new relationships with others. But what is the mountain in your life that needs to be scaled? Without taking the moment of self-examination, it won't be easy to face the challenging mountain before you. It is a crucial step that cannot be overlooked or underestimated, for it can either strengthen or hinder our personal and spiritual growth. If we relate this to unforgiveness, we can see how harboring ill feelings does more harm to us than the other person and hinders our progress. But let's be honest, these obstacles often seem overwhelming. It is easier said than done that we will forgive, let go, and move on. But it is a necessary step in getting your mountains to move. Without pardoning, we cannot experience freedom. However, in this case, it is not the person who did us wrong who is imprisoned; it is us.

Furthermore, we must understand that not all mountains are made of earth and stone; some are built from the burdens we carry within us. Among these, unforgiveness is a formidable mountain peak many cannot overcome. It is a weight that binds us, holding us back from experiencing the fullness of joy and peace. Harboring resentment is a heavy load we were never meant to bear. It is a barrier between us and the divine grace that seeks to renew us. Unforgiveness is also a silent thief; it creeps into the heart, casting a shadow over our relationships and well-being. Just as the unforgiveness I was carrying in my scenario, I was silently robbed of the joy I could have been experiencing with others. I also missed the experience God wanted to have with me.

Therefore, we must look deep within our hearts to unearth any remnants of unforgiveness buried beneath layers of justifications and forgotten conflicts. After all, they attacked me, right? So, don't I have the right to carry this grudge? Yet, harboring such sentiments causes us to carry an invisible burden that weighs heavily upon our souls and hinders our ability to reach the peak of our mountains. Unforgiveness is a mountain we must confront to navigate the path of spiritual and emotional freedom. Because it is a challenge that will test our spirit, resilience, and capacity for forgiveness. And deep within our souls, we must ask ourselves if our hearts are genuinely free from the shackles of resentment. To move forward, we must liberate ourselves from our unforgiveness. We need an act of pardon.

So, before we approach the sacred space of prayer, we must pause and reflect upon the state of our hearts. Prayer is not just a ritual, it is also a communion with God. In this holy conversation, we bare our souls, seeking guidance, strength, and solace. However, to truly stand in the presence of God, we must ensure that our hearts are free of the burdens that weigh us down. There is a warning that is still often overlooked: if the seeds of unforgiveness take root in the garden of our hearts, we are bound by the chains of our misdeeds. The mountain that looms in your path hinders your progress, clouds your horizon, and may very well be composed of the heavy stones of unforgiveness. It was for me. My consequence was that instead of having thoughts of joy and friendships, my heart would be filled with thoughts of revenge. I had a well-thought-out and elaborate plan for getting revenge and getting away with it. It changed who I was born to be, and I did not realize the impact because I felt I had a right to do so. But harboring unforgiveness for years, I was carrying a grudge and an ought against those who did me wrong, and in doing so, I chained myself to the very obstacle I wished to overcome.

Therefore, it becomes imperative that we forgive if we wish to conquer our mountain and experience freedom.

But remember, forgiveness is not merely an emotional release but a spiritual cleansing and a key to liberation. It is a key that unlocks the door to a more profound, more sincere dialogue with God and the ability to experience relationships as they were meant to be. As we forgive, we likely do not forget the hurt, but we choose to rise above it to free ourselves and others from the chains of continuous blame and pain. When we choose to release the grip of grudges, we take the first step toward the summit of pardon. It is a journey that requires courage, for forgiving is not easy. It demands that we confront the pain and the hurt that we have held onto, perhaps even nurtured, over time. Yet, it is essential, for in doing so, we open ourselves to the possibility of reconciliation and healing. This act of courage serves as a declaration that we will not be held captive by the bitterness of the past. It took years for me to get there, but thank the Lord, I'm free! And I believe you can get there too.

So, understand this: forgiveness is not a sign of weakness. It is the hallmark of strength. That thought is especially important for men because the last thing we want to do is portray an image of weakness to others. But the strength to forgive is the key that unlocks the chains of resentment, allowing us to step forward unchained. Let us, therefore, approach the throne of grace with hearts unchained by the shadows of unforgiveness. Let us embrace the liberating power of pardon, for it is in this act of letting go that we find the strength to move mountains and the courage to face the unknown. Listen, choosing to pardon could be our turning point; the moment we choose to release rather than retain, ascend rather than stagnate. Only when we relinquish the grip of unforgiveness can we truly embrace the essence of pardon. It is a transformative process, a metamorphosis that allows us to shed the burdensome cocoon of iniquities and emerge with wings of grace. Forgiving is how we can be set free, to soar above the wild terrain of moral failings, and to savor in the light of pardon and forgiveness.

It's a simple yet challenging formula: Releasing unforgiveness equals freedom. It is an act of pardon that begins within and extends outward. It is a liberating step that allows us to ascend the mountain with a lighter heart and a clearer vision. We open ourselves to the healing and transformative power of forgiveness, a gift we give and receive. Inasmuch, true liberation from our misdeeds requires a profound and all-encompassing transformation.; it demands that we extend the same grace that we seek from above to those around us toward those who have trespassed against us. In my scenario, to this day, there has never been an apology. However, I still had to let it go and forgive. But I have learned that when we release others from the debts of their transgressions, we, in turn, are released. The mountain shifts, and the horizon of spiritual enlightenment broadens before us.

"To be a Christian means to forgive the inexcusable because God has forgiven the inexcusable in you."

C. S. Lewis

Through forgiveness, we mirror the compassion that has been bestowed upon us. Through this act, the mountain of unforgiveness begins to crumble. When we release the grip of grudges, we can genuinely raise our hands to receive the blessings of forgiveness. It is a divine exchange, a sacred transaction where we offer up the weight of unforgiveness to receive the lightness of pardon in return. Now, can you see why self-examination is important? You may feel stuck, and it could be rooted in unforgiveness you may not be aware of, just like it was with me. But I have also learned that through self-examination and release before prayer, we can find the true essence of prayer and the key to unlocking the might that moves mountains. No matter how justified we feel in holding on to the grudge, it is not worth it.

Therefore, we must be courageous in acknowledging our faults, seeking forgiveness, and, most importantly, granting forgiveness to ourselves and others. As we pardon, we find the strength to move mountains, surpass the obstacles of the flesh, and bring ourselves closer to the essence of God. We can also find the true essence of mercy; in mercy, we find the strength to move mountains within our hearts. Let's not carry the weight of iniquity any longer; instead, we carry the grace of pardon and, in doing so, find the peace that passes all understanding. Let's attempt to be architects of pardon and builders of bridges rather than walls. Because when we take down the mountain of unforgiveness, we make way for a horizon filled with hope and new beginnings. Let us rise above the shadows of resentment and walk into the freedom of forgiveness, where the mountain that once hindered us becomes the ground upon which we stand, stronger and more united than before.

The act of pardon and letting go of unforgiveness is vital for our ability to progress forward and get our mountains to move. Again, let us not be mistaken; the journey to forgiveness is difficult. It is a path filled with challenges, with moments of doubt and pain. But it is also a journey of transformation, where each step taken in the spirit of pardon is a step towards the summit of our own personal mountains. In this transformative power of forgiveness, we can discover the freedom that comes with forgiveness, and we learn that sometimes, the most formidable mountain we face is the one built from our own unforgiveness. Sometimes, our enemies are not the other people who did us wrong; instead, they are ourselves because we harbor unforgiveness. And we are creating our own consequences.

Speaking of creating our own consequences, let's consider pardon and forgiveness from an often-overlooked perspective, and this is the reason why this chapter is named "Pardon me?" It is one thing when someone else makes a mistake towards us that creates a mountain because of us holding on to grudges against them, but what about those times when we are the ones who made a mistake? We can be our worst critics, and it can cost us dearly if the poison we have identified as unforgiveness is self-inflicted. In most cases, although letting go of a grudge against someone can be difficult, it is easier than letting go of it against ourselves. It challenges us to look beyond our desire for perfection and admit that a mistake was made. We must learn to pardon ourselves to become unstuck. Sometimes, it is not other people or situations that hold us back; we hold ourselves back.

But there is hope! Regardless of how unmovable and unsurmountable that mountain standing majestically in your way is, it can be moved! And let us also be reminded that the mountains in our lives are not there to defeat us but to be overcome. So, let's be inspired to seek pardon, forgive, and move the mountains in our lives. With forgiveness, we find the strength to climb higher, see further, and live more freely. Let us carry with us the wisdom that we find the true essence of prayer in the act of forgiveness, including forgiving ourselves. For in the act of pardon, we discover the path to true spiritual elevation and the power to say, "I need the mountain to move." And it shall.

> **Did you know?**
>
> Research has been conducted to study the effects of not forgiving. They have found that holding on to grudges can affect physical and emotional health. Research published by Everett L. Worthington, Jr. et al. referenced decisional forgiveness, where we are intentional in our behavior to resist taking a stance of unforgiveness and treat the person who did us wrong differently. Also, there is emotional forgiveness, where we replace negative emotions associated with unforgiveness with positive emotions. Engaging in these two concepts will directly impact our health and well-being. Research such as this helps us understand how grudges hurt us more than the other person.

Let's Put The Work In

How do you feel about forgiving but not forgetting? In this chapter, we discussed the power of pardon and how forgiveness can liberate your mind from the stress that comes with it. The power of pardon becomes influential in your life when you take three steps.

1. **Identify what needs to be forgiven and understand how what happened has affected your life.** Do a self-analysis to compare what happened to your thoughts, feelings, and behaviors. You may find that your character may have changed because of what happened, and others who are not involved may be treated differently. By digging deep, you can better understand how many people are affected by the grudge and unforgiveness you are holding on to.

2. **Motivate yourself to be able to say that you forgive.** This is often easier said than done because when treated wrongly, we tend to feel justified in reacting with a grudge, especially if the person never apologizes. Because we have not received an apology, it is usually the catalyst for grudges and unforgiveness. So, it would help if you resolved that it's time to let it go. If you have identified a grudge, the time to let it go is now. It's challenging and may take time and practice, but you can do it!

3. **Saying you forgive and acting as such are two different things.** When you decide to let it go, saying the words is easy. The hard part is aligning our thoughts, emotions, and behaviors to that act of forgiveness. That act is what creates the power of pardon because of the influence it will have on your life. You will need this influence because you may forgive but will not likely forget. People may say to forget about it, but it's humanly impossible unless you have a condition that affects your memory. However, if our beliefs are aligned with forgiveness, it will influence our thoughts. So, when we see that person, we will think differently now that we have forgiveness in our hearts for them.

Because our thoughts are different, they influence our emotions and behaviors so we can treat that person differently. Before, you may have ignored them or been rude, but now you can engage in a healthy conversation. When it's all said and done, we don't forget, but we react differently when we remember what happened. When you can remember what happened and are around that person again without developing any adverse reactions, you will know that the power of pardon influences your life and empowers you to get unstuck and move mountains out of your way. Think of how the power of pardon can impact your work, family, friends, and community relationships. There is an excellent benefit to letting go.

"Forgiving does not erase the bitter past. A healed memory is not a deleted memory. Instead, forgiving what we cannot forget creates a new way to remember."

Lewis B. Smedes

 ffirmation

I release my burden of unforgiveness and open myself up to opportunities for healing and restoration. I wholeheartedly accept that forgiveness expresses genuine love and freedom for myself. In seeking pardon, I am moving mountains in my life and creating a way for others to find forgiveness. I embrace my ability to forgive, understanding that this strength can be as challenging as moving mountains. Today, I choose to let go of what cannot be changed and find the courage to seek forgiveness as a transformative act of forgiveness.

సౌ

Now, it is your turn to consider your mountain. What would be your affirmation as it relates to pardon and forgiveness?

Action Steps

Once you have focused on what your mountain is, complete these action steps.

1. **Reflect on What Pardon Means to You:** Consider how pardoning can be a transformative experience for both the giver and receiver.
    a. Ask yourself: What does it really mean to forgive?

2. **Reflect on What a Mountain is:** Explore the symbolism behind the mountain in the context of obstacles and forgiveness.
    a. How can moving a mountain compare to overcoming personal challenges relating to unforgiveness?

3. **Identify Your Mountains**: What obstacles in your life do you consider mountains that need to be moved?
    a. How does the power of pardon relate to your mountains?

4. **Reflect on How Pardoning Affects Your Life**: Examine what happens when you pardon someone.
    a. How does it affect your emotional and mental state?
    b. How does it lead to peace and resolution?

5. **Evaluate the Steps to Pardoning**: Outline practical steps that you can take to pardon others.
    a. How would you begin the process, what are the details, and what does life look like after the pardon?

6. **Discuss the Journey of Pardoning**: Forgiving someone may happen in a moment, but it takes time to adjust our minds and behavior to reflect forgiveness.
    a. What are the stages of moving from resentment to forgiveness?
    b. How do you feel about forgiving but not forgetting?

7. **Allow Action to Empower Pardoning**: Remember that pardoning becomes power when we take action. We can't just say we forgive; we must also live it. In doing so, we also serve as an example to others of pardoning and forgiveness.
    a. How can the act of forgiveness be a powerful catalyst for change in your life and the lives of others?

Your turn. After completing these steps, what action steps are still needed for your reflection on unforgiveness?

Prayer

Dear Father, I come to you to honor you. I ask that you help me discover the grudges and unforgiveness I may be holding and accept the seriousness of what I discover. I want to be able to let go so that I can be free to conquer the obstacles in my life. Before I ask for anything, I want to make sure that my heart is pure so that my prayers can also be pure. And when it has been done, when I have been set free, to you be the glory and honor. Amen.

଼

Your turn. What would be your prayer?

"Prayer is the place of refuge for every worry, a foundation for cheerfulness, a source of constant happiness, a protection against sadness."

St. John Chrysostom

Chapter 2: The Power of Prayer

Now that we have self-examined ourselves to ensure that we are not carrying any grudges, unforgiveness, or ought, let us look at prayer's impact on our mountains. Most view prayer as complex; however, it is a simple act, a general conversation between God and us. There is nothing mysterious about it. As we pray, we reveal our hopes, fears, and desires before God. It is a time of honesty, of making our personal petitions known. I remember as a kid being taught the basic prayers such as "Now I lay me down to sleep" or "God is great, God is good, now we thank Him for our food." Prayer became one-sided; I fired off a series of recorded lines and went along my way. But as I got older, my understanding changed as I realized that just as much as I wanted to talk to Him, He also wanted to talk to me.

So it is in these moments that we look for a sign, a whisper, a feeling, or anything to assure us that not only is He listening, but He is also responding. When we pray, we need the reassurance that our words will not go unheard. This is where trying to climb our mountains becomes challenging because we carry the extra weight of doubt. Doubt can set in when we ponder whether our prayers are heard. But let me tell you, just because we may not hear God's voice or see a sign does not mean He is not listening. As a kid, it didn't matter to me. Still, when life presented itself in a way that I needed God to respond to my situations, especially while adulting, I wanted to know that He was also responding as I prayed. But the truth is, even if we do not hear anything or see a sign, God is fully aware of your struggles and concerns.

Imagine when you pray that your prayer is like a seed planted with hope into the ground. The hope is we are anticipating something to grow from that seed and produce fruit, vegetables, or a beautiful blossom. So, think about it: there is a moment in which we cannot see whether the seed is growing. What we do not see is the seed going through the germination process. Under the surface, that seed forms roots and a stem. We do not see this happening, but it's happening. But what happens when the package from which we took the seed indicates that the growth breaks the surface in one week, and nothing happens? These are the moments in our lives that we typically give up. These are critical moments because this is also where we tend to take matters into our own hands, and we feel that God didn't hear our prayer or that He will not answer. However, we must not give up hope and make any adjustments to ensure our seed planted continues to grow at the pace it will take to break the surface to be seen.

It reminds me of a time when I was testing out growing vegetables. I started planting tomatoes. I planted a few seeds, followed the instructions, and awaited the results. Day after day, week after week, and month after month, nothing came out of the ground. Eventually, I stopped checking to see if it would grow. Let's explore this thought because it was not my first time planting tomatoes. I planted cherry tomatoes the previous year and saw the stem break the ground within weeks. Because I had already experienced quick results, there was an expectation that this time would be the same, but it was not. However, one year later, after I decided I was not planting any new seeds, guess what I saw? I saw several sprouts coming out of the ground. My wife's first thought was that weeds were growing. But after time, it was apparent that the seeds I planted a year ago were moving out of the darkness of the ground into the light of day. Remember we discussed earlier that sometimes experience can be a problem? In this case, my experience gave me the impression that I would see the same results, but I didn't and walked away. This is what prayer can be like sometimes; some prayers may see quick results while others may take time. But what we must do either way is not to lose hope that He heard us and is working things out for our good.

See, I had expectations of how the plants should grow. But with prayer, our expectations do not constrain our prayers, and our answers can come anytime. The beautiful thing is God knows what timing is best! He knows how to answer our prayers for our most significant benefit. Can you imagine people watching you struggle in a situation where it seems there is no way out, and suddenly, an open door allows you to prosper? People will naturally be drawn to you to understand what you did to get out of your situation, and that is your moment to plant seeds of hope into them of the power of prayer. So, as we continue to address our mountains with the power of prayer, we must remain hopeful no matter how majestic that mountain is. We may even feel overwhelmed by what we see with our natural eyes. As we stare at life's trials and tribulations, the power of prayer becomes important. Praying and remaining hopeful becomes crucial until we see results and that mountain moving.

Just remember, prayer is not a series of eloquent words or a cadence like we may see in church. Prayer can be as simple as a few words, as in Peter's case. His prayer was simple when he sank: "Lord, save me!" With that simple prayer, Jesus came to his rescue, comforted, and reminded him to keep having faith. Remember that when we pray, there may be no sign or audible voice to confirm that our prayers have been heard or that God is giving an immediate response. But know that the space in between when we pray and when we see results is where our faith is tested. That helps us to understand that prayer is not a magical incantation where we speak things into existence. Instead, it is a declaration of faith, our belief in the power of God to move the mountains in our lives. It gives us a chance to know that no matter how great the obstacles may seem, the power of God is greater than any obstacle we face.

"Prayer should not be regarded as a duty which must be performed, but rather as a privilege to be enjoyed."

E.M. Bounds

Remember, faith is not believing in remarkable things we see with our natural eyes. This is why we should avoid looking for signs. But instead, faith is trusting in what we don't see with our natural eyes, such as with the seed in the ground. We don't see it growing, but we trust that it does. We water and nurture it with the hopes that results will come. Likewise, when we do not see a sign or anything moving with our natural eyes, faith helps us remain hopeful that our prayers have started a chain of events to eventually lead us to victory over our trials, challenges, and obstacles. So, pray with confidence that each word you speak in prayer and each silent thought in your heart is a step towards results, a step towards our mountain no longer being in our way. Know that your prayers are moving or carrying you over the mountain. Your prayer can shake the foundation of that mountain, allowing you to see the horizon again. Just don't lose hope when results may not seem immediate.

Mark 11:20-26 is a passage that captures a moment from Jesus teaching His disciples. It begins with observing a fig tree that Jesus had previously cursed because it was not producing fruit. They were shocked to find a withered tree on their way back. Jesus uses this moment to emphasize the importance of faith. He tells them that if they have faith in God, even as small as a mustard seed, they can tell a mountain to move, and it will obey. Imagine that if faith, the size of a mustard seed, could move a mountain, what would happen if our faith were greater than that of a mustard seed? Furthermore, Jesus emphasizes that when we pray, we should have forgiveness in our hearts, as this echoes the forgiving nature of God Himself. Remember, He wants us to forgive before seeking forgiveness for ourselves. And holding onto grudges or neglecting to forgive others and ourselves can hinder our relationship with God and the power of our prayers.

This passage is a cornerstone for understanding faith, where we understand that faith is not just something we believe in but also an action where we trust that God can provide miraculous results. Let's also consider that just as we learn how faith moves mountains from observing how Jesus commanded the fig tree to be withered, we must also consider the lesson of why the tree was cursed; it was not productive. When we do not apply faith through confidence in what we believe and trusting God, it can lead us to be just as barren as the fig tree. Therefore, the power of prayer becomes manifest when we learn from what James taught us that faith without works is dead.

When we pray, it's not just something where we believe that God will answer that prayer. But our actions and behavior must reflect that we trust Him, even when we do not see immediate results. As with how I treated the cherry tomatoes, I believed they would grow, but I did not take the appropriate actions to ensure they grew. All it took was gentle rain in the appropriate season for the seed to germinate and grow. It was not an immediate response when Jesus cursed the tree. It was when they saw the tree a day later.

So, when we want to activate the power of prayer, the foundation is like faith, which is what we believe. In addition, our trust is the action we must take. For prayer to be effective, we must have both. I can't just plant a seed and not water it and expect it to grow just because I believe it will. I must also abandon what I think I know and adapt to the situation. In other words, treat each prayer as a new opportunity to talk to God. It is a new opportunity to look beyond what we see naturally and trust and believe spiritually in what results God can create. It's also a reminder of other actions to combine with faith, and that is forgiveness. In the previous chapter, we discussed how unforgiveness is a hindrance. Thus, we combine the power of pardon with the power of prayer so that we can see mountains move. The power of prayer is a powerful tool for you to use. It begins with your understanding that prayer is conversing with God, believing that He heard you, and trusting that He will see you through your mountain. Prayer was always intended to be an opportunity to spend time with our Heavenly Father. It is a moment in which we share our hearts with Him, show gratitude for what He has already done, and exhibit faith and trust in what we know He will do. So, when you understand the power of prayer, you can watch your mountain move.

Let's Put The Work In

Maybe at this point in your life, you've felt the power of prayer was more a cliché than reality, or maybe you have already experienced how prayer influences your life. The influence that prayer has on our lives can be transformative. You should pray any time after ensuring your heart is free from ought and grudges. There is no need to wait for a special event or service; you can talk to God whenever and wherever you are. There are some steps you can take to begin to have consistency in your prayer and empower prayer to move mountains in your life.

1. **Remove any preconceptions about prayer.** Eliminate images of how prayer is conducted in a church service or by a charismatic leader. Remember, at its foundation, prayer is simply an open dialogue between God and you. So, don't be afraid to pray if you cannot pray like others; pray like you pray.

2. **Second, remember that if you do not recognize the voice of God, the conversation may feel one-sided.** But although you do not hear an audible response, see a sign, or receive a confirmation, continue to trust that He heard you and is responding either through words or actions. Everyone may describe what it is like to hear God's voice differently. Let that experience be something you discover between God and you; it's personal because it represents your relationship with Him. So, if you cannot say, "I heard the voice of the Lord telling me...." don't feel like something is wrong. Nothing is wrong, so keep praying and talking to Abba, our heavenly Father.

3. **Build a habit of praying every day.** A wonderful time to do this is when you wake up in the morning. Spending time praying before we start our day can influence the trajectory of our day. In other words, starting on a positive note can influence our day to be experienced through a positive filter. Even when challenges come, because we are in a positive mindset, we can approach each challenge confidently rather than allowing it to overwhelm us or cause us to give up. So, pray before you start the day and at any point that you need a little talk with God. Praying at the end of the day gives us a chance to thank Him or seek guidance for what happened during the day. He's always listening!

4. **As we strive not to compare how we pray to others, take a moment to understand what prayer is and how it works for you.** Seek out books discussing prayer and the Lord's Prayer, also called the model prayer, in detail. Take the key points from that and develop a prayer style representing your communication style. Talk to God respectfully. How would you talk to anyone else you love? Don't be afraid to share your heart with Him.

5. **For those prayers, such as when trying to become unstuck and move mountains, write down key points from your prayers.** What you prayed for may come to fruition immediately or take time. Use a journal so that you can come back and reflect on what you have prayed for. You may find some things that have already been answered: a cause for celebration, gratitude, and praise to God. It will remind you of

what you have prayed for and what you trust God to do in your life.

Affirmation

"By praying daily, I transform into the artist of my own reality. By connecting to God and communicating my needs to Him directly, I sculpt away doubt, fear, and obstacles from my path toward my destiny. Faith serves as my hammer while my prayers become my chisel, sculpting pathways through life's challenging terrain - making the impossible possible and insurmountable mountains crumble into steps towards my ultimate destination. As long as I continue praying, my destiny will unfold perfectly for me!"

☙

Remember, prayer not only moves mountains; it gives us hope until the mountain has been moved! Now consider your mountain. What would be your affirmation as it relates to prayer?

Action Steps

While focusing on what is your mountain and how you are feeling stuck, ask yourself these questions:

1. **Reflect on Your Mountains**: Identify the challenges or 'mountains' you wish to overcome through prayer.
    a. What are the obstacles in my life that seem impossible to overcome? How have I tried to overcome them so far?

2. **Understand the Power of Prayer**: Think about how you feel about how the power of prayer can move mountains and the perspective of your faith.
    a. Do you believe that prayer can transform your life by moving mountains? What examples from what you have read thus far resonate with you?

3. **Implement the Lessons**: The book offers actionable advice on prayer, so take note and commit to applying these steps in your daily routine.
   a. Which prayer practices can I start today? How can I integrate these actions into my daily life?

4. **Journal Your Journey**: Keep a journal of your prayer journey, noting any shifts in your perspective or breakthroughs as you apply the book's teachings.

5. **Share, Discuss, and Learn With Others**: Find someone with whom you can discuss the power of prayer and share your experiences.
   a. How do others' experiences with prayer inspire or challenge your beliefs? What insights have you gained from these discussions?

6. **Practice Persistence**: Persistent prayer is vital to consistency in your life's journey. Commit to not giving up, even when the mountain seems unmovable.
    a. When have you wanted to give up on something important? How can you cultivate resilience in your prayer life?

7. **Celebrate Progress**: It is essential to recognize and celebrate any progress or small victories in your journey, understanding that moving mountains can be a process that takes time.
    a. What small victories have you achieved through prayer? How can you use these successes to fuel your continued efforts?

Your turn. After completing these steps, what action steps are still needed for your reflection on prayer?

☙

Prayer

What would be your prayer?

"Do not be anxious about anything, but in every situation, by prayer and petition, with thanksgiving, present your requests to God. And the peace of God, which transcends all understanding, will guard your hearts and your minds in Christ Jesus."

Philippians 4:6-7

Chapter 3: The Power of Petitions

The power of prayer is crucial to our faith walk and helps us on our journey through life. It shows how resilient we can be and gives us hope. When we pray, as we have a little talk with God, there are different things we can say and do. Before we say and do anything, it is good to take a moment to adore Him and thank him for all He has done. Think about it for those who are parents. When your child comes up and starts to flatter you, or maybe they miraculously did their chores without asking and reminding you of what a great parent you are, your first thought is usually, "Ok, they must want something." As funny as that thought is, when we do that with God, it is our way of getting His attention and letting Him know from our hearts how we feel about Him. Once we have given Him His due praise, honor, and gratitude, we can take the time to tell Him what we want.

Depending on what church you've been to, a song just went through your mind, didn't it? However, telling Him what we want is where the power of petitions comes in. Concerning the power of petition, it is more than just asking God to fulfill a request; it is also where we express our desires with determined faith. Therefore, our petitions must be more than words; they must include action. Once again, we refer to James' reference that faith without works is dead. Because it will take more than telling it to move when we reach that point in life where the mountains we are challenged with seem impossible to overcome. We must actively believe it will and adjust our minds and behaviors until it does. Every thought and action we take should align with our faith that what we are asking for will come to pass. Thus, prayer and petition work together because after we have made our request known to God, we need the mountain to move. Prayer keeps us inspired, and we hope that God hears us and is working it out for our good.

So, we find ourselves at a point where we have cleansed our hearts with forgiveness and the power of pardon and have come to God through the power of prayer. We can also petition Him so that our mountain experience's purpose and outcome will be revealed. But it is more than just telling Him we desire to see mountains move; it is a time to share our hearts with Him. It is a time in which we can petition to protect our families, strengthen our community, or help us sleep through the night. Remember, although we are praying to a sovereign king and creator of all things great and small, we are also talking to Abba, a loving heavenly father. Use this time to discuss your life's major mountains, small hills, and speed bumps. Remember, several small hills can be just as challenging as one mountain. So, use this time after we ask for the mountain to move to make a petition so He can guide us in what to do next. After giving our words through faith, we can walk with action regardless of what we see with our natural eyes. Because we may not see that mountain moving, but we trust that in the spirit, God is still moving and has a plan for us.

So, in this interchange between God and us, we reveal our deepest thoughts and feelings to make our requests known to Him. You may say, if He is God, doesn't He already know? Isn't He the omniscient and omnipotent God? And the answer is yes, He does. However, if our existence with Him was God constantly reacting to our heart's desires, would we ever take the time to talk to Him? We would live our lives trusting that he would move it every time we faced a mountain without us ever saying a word. And you know, sometimes that does happen. I can author a separate book on all the times God moved mountains for me, which I never prayed for, but I recognized that it was Him. What I experienced could not be explained by coincidence. Still, instead, it was divine intervention that my fig tree withered, sycamore trees were plucked up, and mountains were cast into the sea. But I could not fall into the trap of believing that God would always do that without me talking to Him.

If we study the bible closely, we'll discover that the children of Israel were trapped in a mindset that if they fulfilled the law and gave their offerings, as long as the high priest initiated atonement with God, they were good. Only the priest went before the mercy seat to speak to God and restore harmony. They were used to Moses going to the mountain to hear from God, and he would repeat what God said. Or they would wait for a prophet to come and share a message with the people. But what wasn't happening was the people wanting quality time with God.

So, when Jesus came, there became an emphasis on everyone having the same access to God so that we could all pray and have conversations with Him. We no longer needed to trust a priest or a prophet alone to do it for us; we could trust God directly. We no longer needed a priest to enact the process of forgiveness. We could go before God ourselves. We can be vulnerable with God and present our needs and wants, knowing He listens to us. It is not just praying and petitioning words into the air. Petitions use faith as a catalyst for miracles, change, breakthroughs, deliverance, and moving mountains. Therefore, the foundation of the power of petition becomes an act where we believe that our request is not just heard but also that our request is being granted. Thus, through the power of prayer and petition, we are not just communicating our requests, but we are affirming our faith that God is more than able and capable of moving mountains. When we believe in this manner, we transform an ordinary request into something powerful, capable of changing our impossibilities into possibilities. It changes and shapes our lives, empowering us to overcome our challenges.

"Faith precedes the miracle. Remember that faith and doubt cannot exist in the same mind at the same time, for one will dispel the other."

Thomas S. Monson

But there is one word that describes what hinders the transformation from impossible to possible: doubt. God does all the challenging work, fights our battles, and works miracles on our behalf. Our job is to conquer doubt. Doubt challenges the power of prayer and petition because it eliminates faith from our petition, which leaves our prayers as just spoken words. In other words, we can't ask and then don't believe in who we're asking and that what we ask for will be granted. Even when we feel He is not granting our petition as expected, we can trust that He answers our prayer based on what is best for us. What do I mean by that? Let's say I am petitioning God to be an instant millionaire, but I have no money management skills. What would be the benefit of Him granting my petition if I am going to waste the money and end up with no money? Based on my opinion, I believe God will grant my petition by giving me a little at a time until I can learn to be a steward of my finances. I would rather not have access to millions until I learn to be a good steward of my finances. I want to be confident that I'll know what to do with it when I have it. That is why I recommend that you not lose hope when our petitions are not being granted in the way we expect. Trust that He is working things out for your good!

However, we also tend to point fingers at other people and even the devil as to why we lose hope. We consider that to be an enemy of our faith. The truth is the greatest enemy of our faith comes from within us in the form of doubt. Doubt causes us to waste our time and God's time. Jesus gave us the point of eliminating doubt and believing in our petitions. In Matthew 11:24, He shares that if we genuinely believe we'll receive what we have requested, we will have our petition honored. But what can we do to win the battle between us and doubt? Our tools for winning this battle include hope and faith. Hope and faith are the power that transforms the unmovable mountain called doubt into a movable mountain called answered prayer. In times of doubt, faith and hope encourage us to trust in what is beyond what we see with our natural eyes and the courage to face the mountains of doubt. Each step taken in hope and faith helps us to chip away at our mountains, creating a path toward reaching our goals.

Hope and faith are what we need if we are going to climb to the top of the mountain or watch God cast that mountain into the sea. Hebrews 11:1 NIV defines faith as "confidence in what we hope for and assurance about what we do not see." When we are unwavering in what we believe, it enables us to move mountains and overcome insurmountable obstacles. Start with faith the size of a mustard seed, and we can eventually cast these mountains into the ocean with our petitions. Faith motivates us to do the impossible and turn hope into reality. We must understand that faith is as powerful as the mountains we face. As a side note, remember that the power of faith is not some mystical force conjured by quoting scripture like a spell or waving our hands through the air. We've watched too many movies! Our mindset has been shaped into believing that faith is an entity or energy, such as with the force in Star Wars.

My point is faith is not a noun; it's not just something you have or know. Faith is more a verb; it is an action we are taking to adjust our mindset to remove doubt and place our hope and trust in God. It shapes our minds to live as if the petition has already been granted. Remember the example I gave about being a millionaire? In this case, it would be me learning how to manage money, how to invest, how to save, and how I will honor God with what He gives me. I would live as if He had given me millions and continue to do so until I have it. What is the benefit? I create a pattern of living based on knowing I can live with a Honda and a three-bedroom. Therefore, when I combine what Paul said, "I have learned to be content," with my new mindset when I get access to millions, I will not rush to a ten-bedroom mansion and a Bugatti because I know those are things I do not need. Just as I trusted God to give it to me, God can trust me to use it wisely.

So, as you face your challenges, remember that petitioning is more than what you know; it is an act of believing in who you are requesting and trusting that He will grant your petition in a manner that's best for you and your future. To believe in the power of God, someone and something we cannot see, with our natural eyes opens the doors by faith to create miracles and move mountains. When asking for something, we create the future we want, one prayer and petition at a time. We can see the reality of our mountains being moved by asking and believing. Your faith can conquer doubt and guide you to see your requests go from being made known to being realized. So, make your petitions known. Speak them out loud and write them down on paper. Write it on a post-it note and place it on your bathroom mirror as a reminder that your petition has been made, then keep your mind filled with hope and faith until you can take that note down, toss it in the trash, and say, "Well, that mountain just got moved! Next!"

Let's Put The Work In

It is common to hear the words prayer and petition and associate them as the same. These were discussed separately to highlight the differences between the two. In simplest terms, prayer is our conversation with God, where we share our heart, emotions, and thoughts with Him and await a dialogue. Petition is where we make our requests to God because it is something we need or want in our lives. They go hand in hand because prayer starts the conversation while we lead into our requests. Think about a child walking up to a parent asking for $20 versus a child walking up to a parent, saying good morning, checking on how the parent is feeling, sharing how they feel with their parent, and discussing how they want to attend a school function. Then, the child says the cost of attendance at the function is $20. The child will have greater success at getting that $20 because they established communication with their parents, and the parent understands why the $20 is needed.

Now, I am not saying that this is some magical formula that will get all your requests granted or that God won't grant a request because you didn't start with a dialogue. What I am saying is that it helps to ensure that when we pray to God, it is not a systematic routine that we do, but rather, we are engaging in a conversation where we share our hearts with our heavenly Father. The power of prayer builds a lifestyle of talking with God daily, even when we do not have any requests. The power of petition reminds us of who our primary source is for getting things done in our lives. Can you see how that applies to getting your mountain to move? Each day, you are discussing your mountain with God. You acknowledge the presence of how great your mountain is, yet in the same breath, acknowledge that God is greater than the mountain. And it doesn't have to be an hour-long process. Here is a quick example.

> *"Father, I come to you knowing you are hearing my heart. Thank you for all the times you have been there for me, and I trust that you are still working things out for me. Your power transcends all power. Your love transcends all love. Although I love you with all my being, it still cannot scratch the surface of how much you love me.*
>
> *I come to you, Lord, because I need you. I need you every day, hour, and second, but I have a problem that must be solved. [Insert problem here] I don't want to lean on my understanding; I want you to guide me. I want to succeed in this because I want you to get the glory out of my life. I believe this problem will be solved, and I will take each step in my life knowing that you are granting my request. I thank you in advance for turning my problem into purpose. Thank you for being Abba to me, and I am forever grateful for all you have done and who you are. In Jesus' name, Amen."*

All it takes is a simple and sincere prayer that we engage in a dialogue, make our requests to Him, and then acknowledge that we have faith, in action, that He will do what is best for us. In it, we have taken the time to show gratitude and exemplify our faith and willingness to trust Him no matter what happens. Here are some steps you can take to help you empower your petitions.

1. **Think about what your request is and try to find scriptures that are relevant to what you are asking God for.** Take a moment to study those verses and meditate on any promises that relate to what you need.

2. **Open your heart to allow the Holy Spirit to guide you.** Remember, the Holy Spirit's purpose is to bring comfort, give you boldness, equip you, and guide you. Trust that the Holy Spirit can guide your action to help take your petition from being words mentioned to mountains moving. Also, be open to corrections or instruction because our plan may not be the best for our desired results. The Holy Spirit connects us to a source of infinite wisdom that can ensure the best chance for success.

3. **Write down your petition.** As we discussed writing down portions of your prayer in the previous chapter, do the same with petitions. God told Habakkuk to take what was given to him, write the vision or revelation down clearly, and inscribe it on tablets so one may easily read it. Habakkuk 2:2 HCSB is translated into different versions of the bible, but the consensus is that it is written down in a way that anyone can read, understand, and be empowered by. See, that is how we go from having a petition to letting the petition be an action. Read it and run with it.

4. **When combining prayer with petition, remember that it should be focused on more than just you.** Not only is this a time that we can talk to God and ask Him to help us, but it is also a time that we can ask Him to help others. We find this in Ephesians 6:18 and 1 Timothy 2:1, which both emphasize making petitions on behalf of others. It allows us to intercede and be our brother's keeper while showing God that we care for others just as we care for ourselves. Can we say, "Bonus

points?" Trust that He will grant your petition for others just as you trust Him to grant your petition for you.

In all things, ensure that you remain confident that God is faithful and that He is listening and eager to grant your petition. Although you may not see the immediate results, praise Him in advance for granting your petition because you know faithfully that He is more than able. Do you see the action in this? Praise God, trust Him, thank Him in advance, and walk confidently as you move toward your mountain, and that empowers your petition to get your mountain to move. You don't have to physically see the mountain moving to know in your heart that it will. So, you need this mountain to move? Pray and tell God about it. Because it is true we cannot move mountains. But we can trust God to move it for us! We are quick to say, "Be gone, satan!" Now it's time to say, "Be gone, mountain!"

"I urge, then, first of all, that petitions, prayers, intercession, and thanksgiving be made for all people— for kings and all those in authority, that we may live peaceful and quiet lives in all godliness and holiness."

1 Timothy 2:1-2 NIV

Action Steps

While focusing on what is your mountain and how you are feeling stuck, ask yourself these questions:

1. **Challenge Unbelief**: Do a self-analysis on what you believe relates to the mountain you need to move.
    a. What challenges, issues, or obstacles are fueling your unbelief?
    b. What in your life do you feel keeps you stuck from believing the mountain can be moved?
    c. What can you do to believe that your mountain will move?

2. **Challenge Doubt**: Reflect if you honestly feel the mountain can be moved.
    a. What have you experienced that has made you believe that mountains can't be moved?
    b. What is in your life that keeps you stuck in doubting that your mountains can be moved?
    c. What do you feel you can do to no longer doubt that your mountains can be moved?

3. **Reflect on Past Prayers**: Remember when you have prayed and asked God for something.
    a. What was your prayer, and what were the results?
    b. How can these results motivate you in your current prayer to move mountains?

4. **Empower Your Petition**: The influence of a petition becomes empowered when we take action.
    a. How can petitioning be a powerful tool for transformation in your life?
    b. How do you feel a petition will aid you in becoming unstuck and moving mountains?

5. **Plan Your Approach**: Reflect on your mountain, why you need it moved, and what impact you want this to have on your life.
    a. Outline what needs to be done for you to consider your mountain to be moved.

6. **Taking Action to Align With Your Petition:** Making your requests known is one thing, but we must also take action to align ourselves with what we are asking for.

    a. What small steps can lead to momentous changes in overcoming your mountain?

Your turn. After completing these steps, what action steps do you feel are still needed for your reflection on the power of petition?

ଔ

Prayer

Your turn. What would be your prayer?

"Knowing trees, I understand the meaning of patience. Knowing grass, I can appreciate persistence."

Hal Borland

Chapter 4: The Power of Patience

What do we do after forgiving ourselves, praying to God, and making our petition known? It is an important question to ponder when we have done those things, yet a mountain still stands in our way. We have asked for the mountain to be moved, yet the mountain is still laughing at us in the face, attempting to show us that it will not be moved. Notice that I use the word "attempting." Because it is our actions that determine whether that attempt will succeed or fail. It is as if your mountain tells you, "Look at what you are going through. Where is your God?" Remember what we discussed earlier: although it may seem that God is not listening to us or doesn't move according to what we ask, it doesn't mean He did not hear us. Just because the mountain doesn't move does not mean that God has stopped moving. But these are moments when the heavens appear silent, when our deepest prayers and petitions seem to disappear in the air, leaving us waiting for a sign or an answer. And that, my friends, is why we must embrace the power of patience.

You know the famous phrase, "Patience is a virtue," right? However, when we feel like nothing is moving, patience is more than a choice; it's necessary. You see, patience does not just mean waiting.

That is typically the definition that comes to mind when considering the word patience. But it is also how we behave when there is a delay. Patience, then, is not just the ability to wait; it is the ability to wait without getting frustrated or complaining. The latter part is vital because being frustrated and complaining that nothing is happening gives way to doubt, and it removes the notion that we trust and believe by faith that God is handling our petition. If doubt is an enemy of our faith, then lack of patience must be doubt's superpower. However, once again, note where the source of this power comes from; it comes from within us. Another person or some evil spirit didn't cause us to be impatient. We chose to give up and complain that nothing had been done.

Think about it this way. Imagine your child asked you for a snack while you were watching a great basketball game. The score is tied with five seconds on the clock. You may think you'll get the snack after those five seconds are up to see how the game ends. But at that moment, your child screams and has a temper tantrum because you have not moved yet to get their snack. How would that make you feel? I mean, you've already decided to grant your child's petition, and you've already decided what snack you will give them. But because you have not moved quickly enough, their emotional state went from trust to tantrum. At this point, some parents would get up to end the tantrum. Other parents may look at the child knowing that if they give in, they create a pattern of behavior in their child that tantrums are what get their requests granted, not trust.

I am not saying God looks at us crazy when we get impatient. But I do believe that it hinders us. Jesus gives us a story, located in Mark 9:14-29, about a father with a sick son who said that the doctors and disciples could not do anything to help him. The father's response was for Jesus to give him something to help him if his son did not get healed. The father is showing us the moment in which he wanted to see his son healed, but because it had not happened yet, he gave up and changed his request from heal my son to give me something to help take care of him as he is. Jesus then pointed out that he was standing before someone who could heal his son, but what good is it if he doesn't understand or believe in who Jesus is? The father changed his mindset with a new petition: help me with my unbelief. And the moment that the father understood and began to have faith and trust, his son was healed; his petition was granted. Thus, when we are being attacked by our disbelief and begin to get frustrated and complain that nothing is happening, we can add a new petition, a petition for God to help us be patient.

Patience resides deep in our hearts, pushing us to suppress feelings that call us towards stress and worry, which come with frustration and complaining. In these moments, patience is our best friend. I admit that this is not always easy, and sometimes, we must deal with anxious feelings. Notice I did not say anxiety. There is a difference between anxious feelings and anxiety. Anxiety is a consistent state of mind and is something that doesn't happen to everyone. However, everyone has felt anxious, especially when dealing with the unknown and unseen. Think about how you felt before getting on a roller coaster for the first time. Or maybe the way you felt on your first date? Better yet, how did you feel when you decided to ask the person

"Patience is bitter, but its fruit is sweet."

Jean-Jacques Rousseau

to go on a date with you? That anxious feeling of nervousness will sometimes prevent us from asking, won't it? Guys, remember the early days in grade school when a girl gave us their number, and how long did it take us to pick up the phone and dial it? I remember picking up the phone and then hanging up over and over. I even remember when a girl wrote her phone number in my yearbook and was too afraid to call. Who knows what could have happened? I'll never know. I share my experience to show how anxiousness can influence us to miss opportunities.

Ladies, remember how you felt while waiting for him to call after you gave the boy the number? Those moments of staring at the phone, waiting for it to ring. Or maybe it rang, and your parents answered it, and you were waiting for your parents to say it was him? How about how it felt when time passed by and he never called? Do you remember the thoughts you had in your head as to the many reasons why he didn't call? Did he change his mind? Is he ever going to call? Did he meet someone else? Did I do something wrong? Am I close to what you may have thought back in the day? Well, this is the same pattern of behavior we can have when waiting for our petition to be granted: we lose patience, get anxious, and give up. We had Jesus on the main line and told Him what we wanted (Do you now remember the song I mentioned earlier?). Yet, it is like He is not returning our call, and we are getting nervous and anxious that He never will.

Let's be honest; we've all had those moments when we asked ourselves, "God, why is it taking so long?" At times like these, we can lose focus and allow logic to take over and rely on what we see with our natural eyes; our mountain is still there. We also will try to use our understanding to solve the problem since it seems God will not do it for us as we asked. Faith, the antidote for the poison of doubt, is the key to staying focused on what you asked God for, even if you cannot see it with your eyes. Also, we must adopt a positive attitude that is steadfast in our faith. I want you to understand how I continue to emphasize the action part of pardoning, prayer, petitioning, and patience, for it is through action that we empower what we know. When patience is transformed into the power of patience, it is more than what we know; it is what we do. It is where we say with a calm spirit, "Lord, I see the mountain through my natural eye, but I believe that you are working spiritually. And by faith, I trust you." Patience will lead us toward perseverance; we can patiently weather any storm. Therefore, we embrace each moment of delay in our petition being granted and realize it allows us to grow in God. And it gives us a chance to strengthen our resolve, build character, and increase our reliance on our heavenly Father.

So, when we have made our request known that we want the mountain we are facing to be moved or for help overcoming the mountain, we can use the power of patience to see us through and have us become greater than where we were before we prayed. It gives us that chance to know that God heard our prayer, granted our petition, and worked things out for our good. If I can pray for a job and get it, pray for a promotion and get it, then what else can I pray for and get in my life? See, it creates a mindset of believing what Jesus wanted us to understand; if we believe, we can have anything we ask for. But we must be patient until we get it.

Being patient shows God we trust Him, enhancing our relationship like the child who wanted the snack. Maybe we decided to give the child a better snack because we were grateful they patiently waited for us to finish watching the game. I believe that is what the power of patience does for us. It allows us to show God that no matter how long it takes, we'll wait on Him and trust He knows what is best for us. Some may think it's about God controlling our narrative. But it is more about developing a mindset that helps us in all aspects of our lives. Imagine if we applied patience to our job and waited for the proper promotion. Or maybe it is patience to wait until the right spouse comes? Or maybe we need the patience to work out our challenges after we get married? Patience becomes the difference between us moving too quickly and missing the proper promotion because we gave up and took whatever was available, and now we're unhappy. Or marry anyone willing, and we feel unfulfilled. And rushing to the courthouse for a divorce before reconciliation can occur. Thus, God allowing us to be in situations where the power of patience becomes necessary is not about Him pulling our strings like a puppet. It is Him giving us a chance to develop and grow into a person who can move any mountain in their life.

Just remember, because your prayer did not immediately come to pass, it doesn't mean God will not move your mountain off your path. We must be patient. We must control our emotions and temper if we are going to be able to show that we trust Him. You can continue to walk forward daily, knowing that God will do what is best for you at the right time. Oh boy, that is another thorn in our flesh regarding being patient. Not only do we trust that God will move, but we must also trust His timing. I would love it to be like what we see on TV; the moment we say what we want, like giving a wish to a magic genie, it instantly appears before our eyes. However, it will not always work that way. There are no special effects, CGI, or artificial intelligence to make all our petitions become immediately evident. Thus, learning to wait without complaining also includes trusting God's timing.

Be patient if it takes ten more years. Hold on until God blesses you. It was 21 years from when I knew I would be an author until my first book was published. It took 26 years for the James Webb Telescope to be approved and the first image to be seen. Imagine waiting that long to see a mountain move. In the case of James Webb, it did, but it took time! So, when you're being patient but experiencing a delay, it is vital to suppress the emotions that make you worry, feel stressed, or complain about your delay. We don't want these emotions to lead to physical or emotional health issues. We want to remain calm, peaceful, and patient until our mountain moves. We won't give in to our anxious feelings because remaining in that state of mind can lead to anxiety. Let us have a healthy experience while waiting for our mountain to move. In addition, let us not give in to logic, lose our focus, and forget the request we made to move our mountain. Instead, we remember what we asked for and that He, who we petitioned, can do everything.

Therefore, let us embrace patience with our whole being and empower our patience with action. Hang on to patience when you face a mountainous situation, when answers are slow to be answered, and the road ahead seems uncertain. The power of patience will help us safely navigate our life's journey as we wait for the mountain to move and allow faith to turn doubt into answered prayers. If we let patience guide us, we will see how the mountains before us can become steppingstones on our journey to higher heights and grow stronger in our resolve. Seeing through the eyes of faith with the power of patience serves notice to our mountain. It is where we can say it like a kid, "I told my father about you, and He's coming, so I suggest you run!" My friend, your mountain will move. Just be patient until it does.

> **Did you know?** *The James Webb Telescope was proposed in 1996. It was not launched until 2021 and did not become operational until 2022. Imagine the amount of patience needed by the founders of this telescope to see it produce its first image. Sometimes, the plans we make may take time. Patience will see you through to the end.*

Let's Put The Work In

"Just be patient" is a phrase we may hear throughout our lives and is often a complex concept to follow in its proper form. The easy part is saying that we have been able to wait. The hard part is that we never complained, became frustrated, or were angry while waiting. That includes times when we must be patient in waiting on someone to do something, such as a family member or friend, or one of the greatest enemies of patience, which is being stuck in traffic. Likewise, we have had frustrations when we have prayed and made our petitions to God, yet we find ourselves still waiting, and nothing seems to be moving; we still feel stuck.

What we would need to do is to learn how to catch ourselves in the moment. At that moment, we are self-aware of our emotions while waiting, and we can take action and empower patience to work on our behalf. For example, let's say we are stuck in traffic because of an accident, and we feel it is about to make us late for work. Our first response is to be led by our emotions, which at this point would be combined with anxious feelings of the consequences of being late, frustration with traffic moving slowly, and anger towards those involved in the accident, which is responsible for this domino effect of emotions. If we live in that moment, it will not only impact our emotional state at that moment, but it will set the tone for the rest of the day. We will arrive at work and begin our duties anxiously, frustrated, and angry. Our co-workers and customers will receive those emotions, which could lead to more consequences.

So, what can be done to change the impact of impatience in traffic? I remember a time after I had just begun to work at a job inside the city of Atlanta. I lived in the metro area, which caused me to commute each day. I knew what driving in traffic was like because I grew up in Miami, Florida. But I was so unprepared for what I would experience with Atlanta traffic. After arriving about fifteen minutes late, I arrived at work flustered and told my boss everything I had seen on the way to work. He just gave me this look like he was saying, "What's your point?" I stopped, took a breath, and he told me he lived near me and knew exactly what I experienced. He finished his talk with a "Welcome to Atlanta traffic."

He helped me to realize this would be part of my daily routine while commuting to work. So, each morning, I would take a deep breath, leave the house earlier, recline my seat a bit, turn on some praise and worship music, and sing all the way to work. I found that I was arriving at work differently and in a more positive mood. Over time, traffic did not bother me as much as it did initially. However, it took time and practice to improve my patience with traffic. Therefore, considering my experience, if we think about the scenario I presented, here are some things we can do to practice patience and change our emotions.

First, let's deal with the anxious feelings. What is the root of the anxious feelings? It is because we are worried about the consequences of being late. What can we do? We can call our supervisor to let them know what is going on. Safely take a picture with your cell phone or locate a news snippet from local news. Be respectful towards who you call. You may want to do a quick breathing routine and speak calmly to avoid projecting your frustrations onto our supervisor. Now that we have covered why we may be late. Let's focus on the next emotion: frustration with traffic moving slowly. What can we do about it? That is both the question and the answer because there is nothing we can do to change the fact that traffic is moving slowly because of an accident. Once again, take deep breaths to try to relax and find something to fill the extra time you have in your car. Listen to your favorite music, something uplifting, peaceful, and encouraging. You may want to avoid music that gets you worked up. While that may be your jam, your jam may add to your feelings of being worked up. At this moment, you want to avoid being worked up and instead find music that brings you down.

And last, let's deal with the anger towards the people involved in the accident. What can we do? Let's begin by realizing that no one wants to be in a crash intentionally (except someone wanting to commit insurance fraud). So, there could be several reasons why it happened, such as debris in the road, someone losing focus, a busted tire, or many other things that could have led to the accident. Let's also consider that people just lost their method of transportation, are going to be extremely late to work, or could be injured, or, worst case, there has been a loss of life. With all those things going on with them, does it make sense to be angry at someone suffering due to something out of their control? Instead, we can pray for them, be grateful for our safety, and take deep breaths to help us relax. Let's replace our anger with feelings of concern and gratitude. This example from my life shows ways we can practice patience. Practice is the key because the more we exhibit patience, the more it transforms us into a lifestyle of patience, whereas our response becomes second nature. By putting it into action, we empower patience to influence how we feel and keep us focused on what we are waiting for. Understand that this is a learned behavior developed and strengthened over time. So, keep at it; you'll get better and get that mountain moved!

Affirmation

"With unfaltering patience, I welcome nature's pace and God's timing of His will as they unfold my path progressively, trusting in each small step taken towards my higher purpose that pushes mountains in my life forward. Through perseverance, I transform obstacles into steps toward my true path forward."

ఴ

Now consider your mountain. What would be your affirmation as it relates to patience?

ఴ

Action Steps

While focusing on what is your mountain and how you are feeling stuck, ask yourself these questions:

1. **Reflect on Impatience**: Identify some moments of impatience in your life and consider the triggers and outcomes of these moments.
    a. How has impatience affected your decisions and relationships?

2. **Understand How Impatience Relates to Your Mountain**: Reflect on how impatience you have experienced may relate to your feeling of being stuck or having a mountain.
    a. How does impatience prevent your mountain from being moved? How do the moments you shared for question 1 make you feel stuck?

3. **Embrace the Journey**: Moving a mountain will not always be an immediate result and will often take time. In addition, some lessons can be learned along the way.
    a. What can you learn from the process of overcoming your challenges?

4. **Develop Mindfulness**: Mindfulness and meditation can promote patience and remain present during the journey. For example, a simple breathing technique can help settle anxious feelings and allow us to stay focused.
    a. Do you feel that relaxing during anxious moments can help you stay patient while waiting for your mountain to move?
    b. What are ways you can incorporate mindfulness practices to improve your patience? (Also consider how you can incorporate it into your daily routine.)

5. **Seek Inspirational Stories**: Draw inspiration from stories of others who have demonstrated patience in adversity.
    a. Which figures in history, or your life, exemplify the power of patience?

6. **Implement Patience Strategies**: Apply practical strategies such as deep breathing, taking breaks, and setting realistic expectations to cultivate patience.
    a. What strategies can you use to become more patient in daily life?

7. **Reflect on Growth**: After applying these steps, reflect on your growth and how patience has contributed to moving your mountain. Revisit this question over time as you practice and improve your patience.
    a. In what ways can I grow through practicing patience?

Your turn. After completing these steps, what action steps do you feel are still needed for your personal reflection?

Prayer

What would be your prayer as it relates to patience?

"You may encounter many defeats, but you must not be defeated. In fact, it may be necessary to encounter the defeats, so you can know who you are, what you can rise from, how you can still come out of it."

Maya Angelou

Chapter 5: The Power of Perseverance

We have discussed different ideas that can become mountains in our lives and prevent us from moving on, leaving us feeling stuck. We feel stuck because our mountain is standing majestically before us, and we don't know what to do. We have learned many ways thus far about what causes us to be stuck. Hopefully, you have noticed some patterns in what we've learned. First, let me continue to reinforce that it will take action. When we take faith from something we know to become something we live each day, we empower forgiveness, prayer, petition, and patience to become a power to move mountains. Remember, power is not what we see on TV. Power more refers to an influence. Thus, pardoning influences our prayers and petitions to be granted, and patience influences our minds as we wait for our petitions to be realized until our mountains have been resolved.

Many things cause us to be stuck while trying to influence our lives to see our mountains move and live in peace. Unforgiveness, doubt, worry, frustration, complaining, and anxious feelings can leave us stuck because they combat the power that comes through pardon, prayer, petition, and patience. And that is where the second thing I want to emphasize is that these feelings of being stuck don't come from other people; they come from within ourselves. Remember, sometimes, we are the mountain that must be moved before another mountain can! To get unstuck, we must focus on what things within us are hindering us from moving forward. Then, we can walk more freely and peacefully as we await for that mountain to be moved or overtaken.

So, it is important to take a moment to assess our situation, not just what is happening around us, just as the story I shared led me to evaluate my life each year. Instead of just recognizing an argument I may have had with someone, I also evaluate what I contributed and what could have been done differently. I develop a plan of action so that if I am in the same situation, I can react differently, hoping for a better outcome. However, that does not come if I continually look externally without taking inventory of what is in me. Someone may have treated me wrong, but I must place a greater emphasis on who I treated wrong. This mindset keeps us ready for life's challenges and allows us to use the power of pardon, prayer, petition, and patience in a way that grudges, doubt, worry, and complaining won't hinder me from seeing my mountain move. In other words, I move myself first to empower my mountain to be moved.

Now that we are empowered by pardoning, praying, petitioning, and patiently waiting, we can also embrace the power of perseverance. Perseverance enables us to keep moving forward and remain steadfast, believing that what we ask for will be realized or manifested despite what we see with our natural eyes. While patience helps us to wait without complaining, perseverance takes that delay and helps us to gain something in our mind and spirit while we wait.

However, perseverance is more than a personality trait. It is a sign of having an unyielding spirit. It says, "I know what I see, but I won't give up! I know the mountain is still there, but I will still go forward! I know the problem is still there, but God is working it out! I may be tired, but I will keep pressing forward!"

We once again understand that it is more than just something we have, but also something we do. With perseverance, we believe that the existence of the mountain is not just there to block us, but we believe its presence tests our strength and resolve. It is a mindset that when we think to ourselves, "I'm not sure I can keep going," we press on anyway, knowing that the mountains in our lives, whether internal or external, will move. I remember when I was in college when my roommate asked me to come to the basketball court to help him practice before the rest of the team arrived. I went, and we took a few practice shots, then decided to do a little one-on-one action. I suddenly remember not being conditioned for that as I had not played in a long time. I was looking for some Gatorade and an oxygen tank! But just as I was about to give up, something in me changed. I was determined to continue, and before I knew it, I was slashing to the hoop and doing reverse layups like I had never done before. I was overpowering him and was scoring at will. Little did I know, the coach had arrived with a few players and was watching. And just like that, although it was not my intention, I had a spot on the team and was given a jersey.

"Going on one more round, when you don't think you can, that's what makes all the difference in your life."

Unknown

That moment would never have come if I had not persevered through that moment of, "I don't think I can continue." Perseverance afforded me something that was not previously available to me. In other words, perseverance opened doors! We went on, and after practice and dedication, we competed and fell one game short of a perfect record. Yep, we lost every game except the team that didn't show up to play us. I don't mind being transparent! Anyway, I shared that to show you how perseverance works. It's a fuel that keeps us going even when we feel we can't. It keeps us trusting even when we don't see the mountain moving. Therefore, let us understand that the mountain does not move because it wants to; it moves because of our faith, patience, and perseverance. Therefore, we must embrace the power of perseverance and understand that when obstacles are not moved immediately, we believe faithfully that regardless of what we see or feel, we can overcome any challenge, no matter how long it takes.

In addition, let's think about a different angle for our mountains that perseverance helps us with. When trying to get mountains to move, we must sometimes embrace why the mountain is there. We may be asking God to move a mountain that was there to protect us from making a wrong decision. Maybe the mountain is there because it is a learning experience that helps us mature, grow, and gain wisdom. The more we understand the mountain before us, the more we begin to reduce its power over us; instead, we hold power over it. Thus, we embrace that perseverance may not be about the mountain moving; it's about climbing over the mountain to help us grow and learn how to overcome life's challenges. It's about believing that prayer and petition will be answered and are within reach if we continue to move, climb, and believe. It's like that old song: it doesn't matter how we get there; we get there if we can.

But to get there, we again must understand that what we need to conquer may not be the mountain we see, but instead, we are the ones who need to be conquered. We conquer by adjusting our mindset and behavior and being determined through perseverance that we've prayed and made our requests known. No matter what happens, we will wait on God faithfully and patiently no matter what. Then, we transform our minds from being hindered and afraid of the mountain to embracing and being blessed by it. Because we know that when that mountain has been moved or if we have been moved to overcome the mountain, we will end up with more than just an answered prayer; we'll also have gained a life experience of knowing that God hears us and moves in a way that it benefits us.

He can do a miracle in our lives in front of others to get the credit and glory because mountains will not move on our own power. It takes divine intervention for miracles to happen. If we went to Mt. Everest and told it to move, would it move? However, if it did, it would not be because we picked it up, moved it, or caused it to crumble. How many people have lost their lives just trying to climb to the top? But if it were to move, then we'd know that it was not our power but the power of God. The power of God is influenced to work in our lives through perseverance because perseverance influences us to keep going and believing until He does His work. We persevere, knowing that if God does not move the mountain, He will take us over it or use it to strengthen us and help us grow.

Therefore, we must realize that we don't always need to overcome our mountains by force or get exhausted trying to find a way around them. We embrace perseverance and the faith that the mountains will reveal and serve their purpose in our lives. Remember, faith and doubt can't coexist when dealing with our mountains. You must choose to allow doubt to paralyze your faith and let your prayers go unanswered or remain just as unmovable as your mountain in your belief and see every prayer answered. Imagine the journey of the James Webb Telescope. It was conceived in 1996 and began operations in 2022. Consider the patience of its creators, who eagerly awaited its first capture of the universe. Through all the decades of approvals, development, design, and deployment, they remained confident that it would produce the results. I am sure that if we studied the history of the progress made on its journey from paper to space, we'd find setbacks, challenges, obstacles, and bad days. Yet, they all worked together and didn't give up until that first image arrived as evidence that what they had believed had come to pass. This is an excellent example of how patience and perseverance work together to produce results. Because even the most meticulously planned plans can take time. Pardon opens the door for prayer and petitions. Patience and perseverance show our faith that God will answer our prayers and grant our petitions. And perseverance will lead us to success. Can you see how that flows to help get your mountain to move? It is a classic case of actions speak louder than words; it becomes a power that moves mountains!

Let us, therefore, persevere. Our consistent commitment allows us to turn the unreal into reality and the impossible into the possible. Look at the difference between the words impossible and possible. To use the word possible, we must remove the "im." I compare this to the word "I'm" to illustrate how we must often remove ourselves from the equation. In other words, we conquer ourselves as to our mindset, emotions, and behaviors before we can conquer the mountain before us. So, let us persevere and believe no obstacle, challenge, or mountain is too big. We maintain consistency through persevering faith that the mountains will shift and the obstacles will fall into the sea. The power of perseverance and prayer is evident when you walk in it. Step by step, we walk with the confidence that every prayer can become a force strong enough to move the ground on which we stand. We walk forward, focusing not on the mountains but on what our life will be like when the mountain has been moved. We also remember that mountains do not conquer us; we are the ones who conquer the mountains. Mountains will always come into our lives. But do you know what? Let the mountains come. Because through the power of pardon, prayer, petition, patience, and perseverance, we are empowered and ready. The mountain will come, and the mountain will be moved. Of this, I am sure. But it is you that must believe it. Do you?

Let's Put The Work In

We often reflect on the scripture in Matthew 17:20, which tells us to have faith in the size of a mustard seed. If you have ever seen a mustard seed, you'll know how small it is. Yet, its small size can grow into something that could grow as high as three feet tall. The point can be missed here because we feel that is the amount of faith we should always have. If a mustard seed is planted in a flower garden, that mustard plant will grow wild and large enough to overtake the other plants in the garden. Isn't it interesting that if I took a larger seed, such as a watermelon seed, the plant would not grow as tall as the mustard plant? In addition, it may take around one hundred days to produce watermelon. In contrast, the mustard plant would take thirty days to produce. Thus, something that started with small beginnings will grow larger and quicker.

Therefore, it is not always about the size of our faith that influences what happens in our lives. We should not always focus on having faith in the size of a mustard seed, but we should also not be discouraged if that is all we must give. It's not the size of our faith that moves mountains; it's the fact that we have it, which casts mountains into the sea. Remember, when we place our petitions into the hands of God, nothing is impossible. However, once we place that seed in the ground, it will not be fully grown the next day. It takes time for the plant to become fully grown and produce fruit. In the process, we must still nurture the plant until it gets there and not give up on nurturing actions until the fruit has been produced and harvested.

Does that sound familiar? If it doesn't, then go back and reread this chapter. Because what it takes in the thirty days of waiting for the mustard plant to produce fruit is perseverance. Remember, perseverance is what we do while being patient, and the power keeps us going forward, anticipating our desired results. It is the power that keeps us from giving up. If I wake up the following day and do not see a sprout from the mustard seed and give up, there is a chance that it will never grow and that I will never get the results from what I planted. This is because I didn't nurture it, such as watering it, feeding it, or ensuring it gets the appropriate amount of sunlight. Likewise, when we have made our petition and are patiently waiting, we must take action to remain steadfast until we reach our goals and our mountains have been moved.

First, we must adjust our mindset to stay focused and positive while waiting for our mountain to move. Think about the story of the James Webb Telescope we've discussed. Imagine if they felt that it was too much at some point and gave up because it was taking too long. We would never have seen the images that it has given us today. We must maintain a level of persistence and refuse to give up. This is where writing down our petition helps because we can revisit it to help remind us of why we are waiting: to see that mountain move. When writing down your petition, remember to write a statement that frames your life once that mountain has been moved and stay focused.

Next, make sure that what you are trying to accomplish is realistic. Moving a physical mountain may be unrealistic, but overcoming fear is realistic. Changing habits is realistic. So, if you have been completing the work in this book, you have created a plan, and within that plan, you should have outlined steps and strategies to help accomplish each step. Make sure that what you have written is realistic. Here is what I mean. If I need more finances, which sounds more realistic, choosing a savings plan or robbing a bank? Think about it about the power of petition. The difference would be, "Lord, help me to manage my finances in a way that I promote savings," verses, "Lord, help me to rob this bank without being caught." If you choose the second option, you'll need to learn to persevere while waiting to be released from your prison sentence. But if you choose the first option, then with actions taken, you can perseveringly adjust your finances and see the results in your savings account over time. Thus, ensuring that your goals are realistic helps to ensure positive results and celebrate when you see them!

And last, learn from what happens while being perseverant. After all the years of waiting and finally having the James Webb telescope constructed and ready for launch, they faced several delays due to issues with the propulsion system, COVID-19, other technical issues, and weather conditions at the launch site. Through all the delays, they were finding issues and learning from them. For example, in 2016, testing was done on the effects of vibration, and it was deemed acceptable. There was another delay in 2021 because of vibrations. Imagine if they had given up because of finding more vibrations? However, they overcame that issue, resolved all other issues, and persevered until the launch vehicle was ready and the weather cleared for launch. Construction was completed in 2016, but delays moved the launch to December 2021. Five years of persistence and perseverance influenced getting the telescope in space and operational. So when we have setbacks, let's not give up.

But instead, let's learn, adapt, and keep going until that mountain is moved!

Affirmation

"I know I possess the strength within me to overcome any obstacle. By leaning on faith and determination as guides, I will transform barriers into bridges and mountains into pathways. Every challenge presents an opportunity for growth that brings me closer to my ideal self."

☙

Now consider your mountain. What would be your affirmation as it relates to perseverance?

☙

Action Steps

While focusing on what is your mountain and how you are feeling stuck, ask yourself these questions:

1. **Set Clear Goals**: Refer to your plan to "Plan Your Approach" in Chapter 3, The Power of Petitions. Each step you create is a goal towards becoming unstuck and seeing your mountain moved.
    a. What can you do to ensure that you persevere to make it to each step?

2. **Engage with the Content**: You have read five concepts of helping to move mountains and remove feelings of being stuck. Take a moment to reflect on how it relates to your life.
    a. Which aspect of this book inspires you the most?
    b. <u>Optional</u>: Email me your response at mountains@kelvinpendleton.com. Include a statement granting me permission if you'd like me to use it publicly.

3. **Reflect on Your Growth**: If you have been completing the work after each chapter, pause to reflect on how these concepts, pardon, prayer, petition, patience, and perseverance, are evolving within you.
    a. How have you grown or changed in your understanding of your mountain?

4. **Share Your Insights**: Discuss the book with friends or in a book club. Sharing your insights can deepen your understanding and inspire others.
5. **Revisit and Re-evaluate**: Perseverance is a journey, not a destination. Revisit the book after some time has passed and evaluate your progress.
    a. How have my views on perseverance and overcoming challenges changed since reading the book?

6. **Pay It Forward**: Use the book's inspiration to encourage others. Your experience could be the push someone else needs to move their mountain.
7. **Empower Perseverance**: Reflect on perseverance and how it relates to your effort to get unstuck and move mountains.
    a. What strategies can you use to enact perseverance until your mountain moves?

☙

Your turn. After completing these steps, what action steps do you feel are still needed for your personal reflection?

☙

Prayer

What would be your prayer?

"One who can move mountains starts with the little stones."

Confucius

Chapter 6: The Power That Moves Mountains

You probably began reading this book with the idea that you have many external mountains to overcome. However, now you should understand that the mountain inside us is more important. That is why self-analysis and being self-aware of our beliefs, thoughts, emotions, and actions is essential. By conquering our inner mountain, we can be unmovable in the face of our external mountains. We can become as immovable as the mountains we face by empowering pardon, prayer, petition, patience, and perseverance through action. As we consider the mountains we face, we must use our wisdom and discernment to help us overcome them or watch them move out of our way. Thus, ask yourself, "What is my mountain?" Your mountain may be something that must be conquered or moved. In other words, is it there to hinder you, or is it there to strengthen you?

Some people have a mountain deeply rooted from within, a personal obstacle that appears to keep us stuck and grounded. This mountain is a test of self-awareness. It allows us to evaluate our lives to remove things that hinder and hurt us, such as grudges, anxious feelings, worry, doubt, frustration, and complaining. These things poison our prayers, faith, and physical and emotional health. Therefore, realizing that the journey may not always be about conquering mountains but rather about growth and introspection is essential. It is about the inner battle no one can see but God and us that needs to be won. Self-analysis, courage, faith, and hope are required to know how to deal with the mountain that is within us. Because to conquer the inner mountain, we must overcome our fears and insecurities. As I shared at the beginning of this book, we must look at the mountain and learn what it takes to climb and conquer it. It is a time when we learn climbing techniques and what gear we should take that is relevant to that mountain. Likewise, when we look within ourselves to our inner mountain, we learn about what it is and what we'll need and then find the strength necessary to climb it. Instead of blaming others as a tool for this mountain, we allow ourselves to be transformed into who we need to be to handle our external mountain.

Then, we can look outward and see the mountain before us. The external mountains represent the challenges we have throughout our lives. The tests, trials, tribulations, and consequences of our actions are sometimes evident to everyone. And it is in these moments that if we allow patience and perseverance to do what it needs to do, it allows God to work miracles in our lives in front of everyone so that they can also know that God is willing and able to do all things. The problem is, in reference to the story of Jesus and the fig tree, we walk up to the fig tree and mountain without understanding that Jesus didn't say that a few things we ask will get answered. No, He said that whatever we ask, if we remain consistent in our faith, our petition will be granted. So, not some things, but all things. I imagine that neither Jesus nor those traveling with him was thinking about that fig tree until they returned to it and saw that it had withered. That is the same way we need to allow our petitions to become evident; through patience and perseverance, we can move forward with our lives without worry and doubt, knowing that God will move. All we must do is actively trust Him and return to see that fig tree withered, to see that mountain plucked up and cast into the sea.

You must have the wisdom to understand what you should do about your mountain, whether internal or external. Discern the purpose of the mountain in your life and embrace it. I doubt that a person has just walked up to a rugged mountain and begun to climb it successfully. Instead, they first acknowledged the presence and magnitude of the mountain. They carefully planned each reach and step taken to scale to the top of the mountain. Thus, if the mountain is inside you, know what needs to be done to conquer that mountain so that you will be strengthened to conquer external mountains. If you have not conquered doubt, you will find it hard to see that external mountain move because you'll likely give up before it happens. Removing doubt and worry allows patience and perseverance to carry you until you are over the mountain or the mountain has been moved.

"If doubt is challenging you and you do not act, doubts will grow. Challenge the doubts with action and you will grow. Doubt and action are incompatible."

John Kanary

Consider this: maybe the mountain in your life will make you pause, reflect, and reassess where you are and where you want to go. You may not be stuck. It could be God preparing you for the next step. As we face our mountains, embrace the wisdom of knowing our path, faith in walking it, and perseverance in believing we will eventually see the mountain moving even if we don't see it happening. When we do this, it is not only the mountain that is moving, but we are also moving. In addition to our mountains being transformed, we are also being transformed in our minds, faith, and endurance. The more mountains we conquer, the more we are transformed and ready to face whatever comes our way; we become more than a conqueror.

When we hear the word "transformation" being used, it is not that we are physically becoming a new person. Instead, our mindsets change. We used to face life with doubt, but now we face it with faith. So, the mountain may not hinder us but transform and shape us and teach us our resilience and faith. In this case, the mountain moves us even as we try to move it. Therefore, the mountain is an integral part of our story and a catalyst for strength and growth. In other words, the mountains are obstacles and opportunities to grow, reflect on our lives, and prepare ourselves for more incredible things. We must all have the courage and faith to say, "I want the mountain to move," and persevere until we see it happen.

The Gospel of Mark chapter 11, verses 20 to 26, reminds us of the power and importance of forgiveness, faith, and prayer. Jesus uses the example of the fig that withers at the command to faith. He teaches us that we can have what we pray for if we believe. But He also stresses the importance of forgiveness because if we keep grudges in our hearts, how can grace be received? This story is a constant reminder to us in our daily lives that our mountains aren't impossible nor immovable, for with God, all things are possible. We can face any mountain if we have a heart that forgives (pardon), a spirit that seeks (prayer), an urge to ask (petition), contentment with waiting (patience), and a determination to remain consistent no matter what (perseverance). And by doing this, our mountain and our journey will not mold us into something we are not; we will mold our mountain and our journey because of who we are in God.

Hopefully, you have taken the time to complete the sections and put the work in. Don't let this only become a book you read; instead, it is something you took action with. That is where the power comes in: through your actions. Remember, it is not about waving a magic wand but taking action to help conquer inner and external mountains. After all, sitting with no action is why we are stuck. We can remove the adverse effects of holding grudges and unforgiveness through the power of pardon. Not forgiving does not hurt others; it hurts us the most. So we can liberate our minds and allow us to live in peace. Through the power of prayer, we can instill hope in our lives.

Having hope for tomorrow helps us to have something to look forward to. It gives us something to smile and laugh about. It helps us to live in peace. The power of petition helps us never forget what we need: to know that someone is listening and that we are not alone in our struggles. It lets us know that we have help in our lives and helps us to live in peace. The power of patience helps us remove worry and stress, which can lead to other physical and emotional problems, allowing us to live in peace. The power of perseverance helps us continue to march forward, even if we still see the mountain, to know that when we reach that mountain, it will be moved, or we will be carried over to overcome it. It will allow us to be wiser, stronger, and more resilient. And that will allow us to live in peace. So, maybe in addition to telling our mountains to move, we need to tell ourselves, "Peace, be still." Because instilling peace within ourselves can influence peace in the environment around us.

See, all I have shared in this book was not just something I made up to sell a book. This comes from my life experiences. I have shared real, biblical, and hypothetical stories to show how they compare to real life. So, when people see me and wonder why I look so peaceful, I have learned to forgive. I remember to pray. I ask God for His help. I patiently wait until He helps me. And I persevere until that Helps transform my mountain into my tool. When I was growing up, we would have appliances fail, such as washers, dryers, and refrigerators. When it was time for us to replace it, I would hear my dad say this irritating phrase, "I'm going to wait on the good Master." Wait on the…what? Man, we need to wash clothes! These are the thoughts that would go through my mind. But over time, this is something I learned from my dad. Each time, he would find this incredible deal. It may be a sale at a store or an estate sale where someone is moving and selling items from their home. We needed a washer; instead of paying $500, he may have only paid $50. He prayed with a pure heart, letting God know what He wanted. He patiently waited, never complained, and persevered until the mountain was moved; prayer granted. Thus, I learned from that experience to do the same, to wait until God has moved and guided me to the solution to my problem because He knows what is best.

This tool of pardon, prayer, petition, patience, and perseverance strengthens my resolve and relationship with God. I know He's moved mountains in my life, both seen and unseen. He has made ways out of no way! Seeing Him move mountains yesterday gives me hope, faith, and assurance that mountains will also move tomorrow! I learned to understand what "Wait on the good Master" means and have reaped the benefits just like my dad has time and time again. Now it's your turn. I believe God can do it for you because He's done it for me. While I may intercede for you, you must still believe that you can get this mountain to move by trusting God. When you have discovered how to move yourself, you will see that you can move mountains. Now go, don't just tell it on the mountain; tell that mountain to move!

Let's Put The Work In

I look forward to hearing your praise reports. I know what I have shared is true, not because I came up with fancy words but because God has done this with me repeatedly. His Word is true to me because He has worked His Word through my life. I have had my mountains, and I have had my mountains to move. I used to think I had to climb them, but now I understand that I must ask God to move them, and He'll move them. Or maybe I need Him to reveal its purpose, and I'll grow and transform from it. Whatever you are going through, no matter what you are waiting on God for, pray until that mountain moves in Jesus' name! When we emerge on the other side, we will not only have moved mountains but also have transformed ourselves in the process. Your future awaits you! But first, you need those mountains to move!

With each chapter, work was to be done that reflected upon the chapter's topic. This time, I am leaving you a blank canvas for you to create your own action steps. Here is a blueprint you can use each time you feel you have something that has you stuck and you want the mountain to be moved. By using this, you can create a plan using what you have learned to find success in getting mountains to move. Whether it be an inner or external mountain, the best way to overcome the mountain to get unstuck is to ensure you have a plan. Most of us fail to reach our goals because we place our focus on the goal and neglect the journey. It is like walking toward a mountain, constantly staring at the peak, imagining what it will be like when you reach the top of the mountain, but failing to see that your next step is an area of quicksand. Before you know it, you're stuck and can't move.

So, you must pay attention to each step required to reach the top of the mountain and handle each step. Each step is a win towards the final victory of reaching the mountain's peak. Taking the time to celebrate each step can help you build momentum. Think of it like being in college. The goal is to graduate with a degree, but each class you take is a step toward that goal. Every time we pass a class, excitement goes along with completing the class, and we begin to count down how many classes we have left. Every time we pass a class, we ride the momentum to the next class, which motivates us to want to continue excelling in classes. However, think about how it feels if we fail the class. There is a gloom associated with failing a class because we realize that we cannot reach graduation without passing specific classes and earning the required credits toward graduation. This is the moment that some contemplate dropping out of college, feeling they cannot do it.

This example shows why preparing for the journey is more important than focusing on the goal. We must anticipate that each class will present challenges that we must adapt to overcome. When we make mistakes or fail a class, we learn what it will take to bounce back. If we fail a class, we can retake it, knowing what to expect from the class. We can speak with professors to learn what we can do to improve. We can talk with classmates who passed to gain understanding from them. There are many things we can do to prepare us better to pass the class when we retake it, and passing the class places us back on track to graduation.

This is the same that applies to life. We must be prepared that each step will present us with challenges. Some challenges will be the same, and others will be different. Here is another analogy to help understand how steps can change. Consider a couple that just met and started dating. This step is about getting to know one another and assessing compatibility. Once the proposal is given and accepted, the steps change. It's about preparing for a wedding and starting a life together. Once the "I do" and rings have been exchanged, the steps change to merging their lives under one roof, combining possessions, merging finances and expenses, and learning to make decisions together rather than as individuals. Then, remember the phrase we used as kids, "First comes love, then comes marriage, then comes a baby in a baby carriage." Suddenly, with all the effort they have put into learning each other, merging their lives together, and placing energy towards focusing on each other, they must figure out a way to share that energy with a baby. How can they make the baby the center of attention without feeling the effects of losing attention from each other?

I could go on and on in this analogy, but can you see the progression of challenges? In each step, failure could cause the relationship to end. However, learning to overcome mistakes is what keeps the relationship intact. But if they were to only focus on the fairytale goal of getting old together, they would miss the opportunity to safeguard their relationship by planning each step or change in their lives together and working through every challenge to avoid walking into quicksand. This applies to relationships, careers, ministry, personal development, friendships, etc. (Maybe I should write a marriage edition of this book).

If I only think about sitting at a table outside a French café looking at the Eiffel Tower and never make plans for each step to get me there, I'll never get there. It will all just be a dream, and I'll be stuck in the woods of Georgia. However, suppose I make a clear intention to get there, develop a realistic strategy, gather all necessary resources, execute the plan, monitor the plan, and celebrate each time I accomplish a step or task toward the primary goal. In that case, I will find it easier to get there and can avoid stepping into metaphoric quicksand. So not only can we use this to get unstuck, but we can also never get stuck again.

Maybe you have read all the chapters and are thinking about how these principles relate to being stuck. So, let's look at it in reverse order. If we do not persevere, it will lead to us being impatient. If we lose patience, it hinders our petitions because we give up and lose hope. How do we get things done if we don't make a petition? When we pray, we would never ask God for help. How can we cultivate our relationship with God if we do not pray? How would we learn to hear His voice? If we don't forgive, not only does it poison us, but it hinders us from seeking forgiveness from God when we make mistakes. Hence, we try to make moves in life, and we get stuck. We are stuck because we try to pray, but our hearts are clouded with unforgiveness and leave us in an unforgiven state when we make mistakes and try to seek harmony with God. Our emotions and mindset remain stressed, worried, doubted, fearful, and hopeless. Do you know what these emotions can lead to if we stay in that emotional state? Depression and anxiety if we are not careful.

Because we have not made it through these steps, we never get a chance to see God move. We miss opportunities to understand He is real and experience Him as Abba. We may even turn away, thinking this whole idea of God is nonsense because we've never seen Him move in our lives. When obstacles, challenges, tests, and trials come as a metaphoric mountain, we immediately feel nothing can be done. It becomes the root of our belief system. That root keeps us grounded in the same place because of how our beliefs influence our thoughts, emotions, actions, and environment. But with each step, we can get uprooted, move out of the quicksand, and progress towards our mountains. We heal ourselves by letting go of grudges. We put the work in to make a wholehearted effort to heal our hearts by forgiving others, whether they apologize or not. We will no longer let unforgiveness poison us and keep us from reaching our full strength and potential; we will rise and ascend our mindsets! Then, we can approach God in prayer with a pure heart and have confidence in knowing that someone is always listening to us; we begin to experience the idea that we are never alone, which reassures us. Every negative belief, thought, and emotion can be laid before Him as we realize He is the best counselor in the world who will listen and comfort you. His comfort can relieve our stress and worry.

Removing these emotions can help pull us out of depression. We can get things moving again because we can petition God. As we see Him work, we get reassurance that He is not only listening but is taking action to bring positive change in our lives. Seeing Him move relieves feelings of doubt because we realize that all things are possible with Him. Our hope is restored because He reveals how He desires to be a part of our progress toward greater things. He doesn't want us to be stuck. He doesn't want us to be filled with anxiety or depression. He wants us to be free! So, we learn to be patient because whether we hear His voice, physically see Him moving, or still stare at our mountains, we have faith that He is faithful. So, no matter what, we continue to press forward with perseverance, determined to see His mighty hand either move our mountain or carry us over it, taking us to higher heights in our growth, character, and strength.

Thus, our beliefs that were once rooted in stagnation are now rooted in faith, hope, endurance, and determination. Not only does the mountain in your way move, but every mountain formed against you will never prosper if you keep trusting and believing by faith. Can you see the difference and progression from being stuck to unstoppable? Imagine living a life where no obstacle, test, trial, or challenge can stop you! The catalyst is that we take actions to forgive, clear our hearts, pray, bear our souls, petition, ask for help, be patient, know He is going to see us through and persevere because we know He can do all things. Faith and hope then transform from something we have to something we live. Faith and hope become our tools to ensure fear, worry, doubt, and stress never get the best of us, and because of this, we understand there is no need to fear. Without these negative emotions, not only do we combat the things that keep our mountain in place while we sink in quicksand, but it removes us from the emotions of depression and anxiety. Our steadfast and active faith, hope, and determination empower us to become steadfast when challenges try to stop us; instead of our mountains moving us, we move the mountains!

These principles not only move mountains but also heal us internally when our internal mountains have been moved. Moving our internal mountains empowers us to face our external mountains with the confidence of knowing that no matter how tall, how majestic, how wide, or how long the mountain has been standing there, it doesn't stand a chance against a free and healed version of us full of hope, faith, and steadfast determination that it will no longer hinder us in life. Because we've cleared our hearts and done a self-analysis to become self-aware of our internal and external mountains. Then, we move our internal mountains with faith, hope, and steadfast determination in action. At the same time, God moves our external mountains with His actions of miracles, healing, and breakthroughs. We move so that He can move. Thus, transforming our mindset to believe in His ability allows Him to transform our lives. And that, my friends, is liberating!

Mountains will still come and stand in our way. Still, we approach the mountain with a different and transformed mindset because we have the confidence that we have analyzed ourselves, our situation, and what stands in our way enough that we know what plans we need to make to see that mountain move. We also must understand that the power to move mountains comes when we act on what we understand. We often get stuck because we do not recognize the actions we must take to make progress in our lives. Knowing the definition of patience is not as powerful as putting it into action. We must learn how to transform our mindsets from nouns to verbs and transform what we know into what we do. Then, we can build confidence through faith that we can do all things because we believe He can do all things. And it is when you find that steadfast confidence through faith that each time, you can continue to say, "Let the mountain come because I am ready to move it!"

When editing this book, I used Google Gemini to ensure that the subtitle was impactful from a marketing perspective. The two choices I wrote were "Discovering the Power to Move Mountains" and "Discovering the Power to See Mountains Move." I contemplated using the second option until the comparison revealed that one evoked a feeling of observation, "See Mountains Move," while the other evoked a feeling of action, "Move Mountains." I wanted to share that to reinforce the idea that we only get the mountain to move through action. The fact that you're reading this book shows what happens when you don't give up on your dreams because I could have given up long ago. So don't posture yourself to see the mountain move; posture yourself to move the mountain through faith and action based on the principles discussed in this book. I hope and pray that you have not just read this book for enjoyment but have taken the time to reflect and put the work in to see things happen in your life. I celebrate in advance for you to no longer feel stuck and for seeing your mountains move!

ffirmation

After completing the book, what would be your final affirmation for yourself from now on?

Action Steps

Use this as a blueprint. This book has asked you many questions to help you reflect on your mountain, and I hope that even now, you may be thinking that you've already seen your mountain move. The following questions can serve as a foundation for making an action plan, and I would encourage you to use them for each action step.

1. **Reflect on Your Inner Mountain**: Before tackling any external challenge, understand the personal beliefs and fears that form your inner mountain. Ask yourself: What limiting beliefs are holding me back?
2. **Set Clear Intentions**: Define what moving the mountain means to you. Is it overcoming a personal obstacle or achieving a goal? Please write down your intentions to solidify them.
3. **Develop a Strategy**: Reaching the peak requires planning like any mountain expedition. Outline the steps you need to take to overcome your inner or external mountain.
4. **Gather Resources**: Identify the tools, skills, and support systems you need. Consider what knowledge or assistance will help you on your journey.
5. **Take Action**: Begin with small, manageable steps that lead to more considerable changes. Each step forward is progress up the mountain.
6. **Reflect and Adjust**: Regularly assess your progress. Are your actions moving you closer to your goal? If not, what adjustments can you make?
7. **Celebrate Milestones**: Recognize and celebrate when you have accomplished an achievement. Each success is a part of the more extensive journey to move your mountain.

Steps to Take Next:

1. Identify one limiting belief and take action to challenge it.
2. Reach out to a mentor or support group for accountability, guidance, and encouragement.
3. Create a vision board representing your journey beyond the inner mountain.

༄

I thank you for purchasing this book and for reading this far. I hope and pray it will be a blessing to you in a way that you see progress in your life. It would help if you did not feel that what I have shared is the only thing that stands in our way. But it serves as a blueprint to start the process of self-awareness so that you can discover within yourself what may be holding you back. It may take asking someone you trust to mentor you through this process or using a coach or counselor to guide you through conversations to help you discover your quicksand. So, do not be afraid to get help, especially in cases of depression and anxiety. Also, as you read this book, I am already writing part two! In the next book, you will learn how elements of our past have created limits in our lives that hold us back. As I mentioned, this book does not cover every factor that may make us stuck. So, I want to share a few more factors because resolving our past is a fantastic way to ensure we can move forward. Stay tuned because I want your mountain to move, and now it is up to you to get it done (and get a copy of the next four books in the Moving Mountains series). Now go, move that mountain! And remember, mountains won't move until you believe that they will! You are never alone! You got this! It may not feel that way today, but tomorrow, you will win! We ride at dawn! Let's go!

Acknowledgments

The photos used in this book were obtained from Unsplash per its usage license and terms and conditions. I want to credit and honor them for their talent and craft, and I am grateful that they share their gift with the world.

Book cover: Photo courtesy of Leio McLaren.

Preface: Photo courtesy of Joshua Earle
Chapter 1: Photo courtesy of Jon Tyson.
Chapter 2: Photo courtesy of Ben White.
Chapter 3: Photo courtesy of Ivana Cajina.
Chapter 4: Photo courtesy of Austin Prock.
Chapter 5: Photo courtesy of Jason Hogan.
Chapter 6: Photo courtesy of Killian Pham.

I want to thank Kirby Love (www.ghfgd.com) for holding me accountable for completing the manuscript according to my goals and providing guidance on marketing this book. His life is a reminder to go hard for God daily; it's a lifestyle. I also want to thank Rory Cordon Edge for reigniting my desire to publish my first book through his book author seminar. He helped me stay focused on ensuring that my books are intended to change lives, enable people to grow, enhance others' identities, and bring others closer to God. I also want to thank Asha Cannon, owner of The Lovejoy Publishing Company (https://thelovejoypublishi.wixsite.com/lovejoy), for providing valuable inspiration and information on publishing this book. Watching her move is an honor and a privilege.

I can't wait to see these names on the national stage! Can I go deeper (In my DeCarlo Marcus voice)? I can't wait to see these names on the international stage! Yes, I said it!

About the Author

Kelvin Pendleton is a licensed and ordained Christian Minister and a President's List student working towards a master's degree in clinical psychology specializing in Clinical Counseling. He aims to become a Licensed Professional Counselor to help his community and, through advocacy, bridge the gap between clinicians and the church. In addition, Kelvin is passionate about helping individuals transition from one stage of life to another through personal, professional, and spiritual development. He is a licensed and board-certified life coach. He operates Kelvin Pendleton, LLC (www.kelvinpendleton.com), doing business as the Pendleton Development Team, which provides life coaching, training, and development services.

Kelvin also earned three bachelor's degrees in information technology, divinity, and Christian leadership, specializing in advanced biblical studies. He has been a servant in ministry for over 28 years, including Christian counseling, teaching, motivational speaking, leadership training, and ministry development. He is a member of the American Association of Christian Counselors, International Christian Coaching Association, American Psychological Association, American Counseling Association, Psi Chi Honor Society, and the National Society of Leadership and Success.

Kelvin Pendleton has been writing for decades through blogs, poetry, and songs and is finally becoming a published author. Kelvin has mentored and/or trained other leaders, including Pastors in India, Kenya, Nigeria, Togo, and the Philippines, using his background in technology to reach others, conduct ministry, and train. Kelvin Pendleton's vast professional and ministry experience spans leadership, Christian counseling, life coaching, educational roles, motivational speaking, leadership mentoring, and developing ministry programs and business processes. However, his favorite leadership role is leading as a husband and father. He is a loving husband to a beautiful and successful wife, Alisa, father of one handsome son, Joshua, and one beautiful daughter, Gabrielle, and devoted to family. Eager to impart wisdom, provide guidance, inspire, uplift, and educate, Kelvin is a constant presence in leadership, whether in his professional environment, religious communities, or civic engagements. Driven by purpose, he offers insights to those eager to engage with his work or seek counsel.

I Need This Mountain to Move
Companion Workbook
Be sure to grab a copy of the workbook. It will allow you more space to write out your thoughts, and there is bonus content to help you "put the work in."

ISBN: 979-8-9910469-2-3

www.ingramcontent.com/pod-product-compliance
Lightning Source LLC
Chambersburg PA
CBHW050649160426
43194CB00010B/1871